Roman Farm Buildings in Italy

J. J. Rossiter

BAR International Series 52
1978

B.A.R.

B.A.R., 122 Banbury Road, Oxford OX2 7BP, England

GENERAL EDITORS

A. R. Hands, B.Sc., M.A., D.Phil.
D. R. Walker, M.A.

B.A.R. International Series (Supplementary) 52, 1978: "Farm buildings in Roman Italy."

© J. J. Rossiter, 1978.

The author's moral rights under the 1988 UK Copyright,
Designs and Patents Act are hereby expressly asserted.

All rights reserved. No part of this work may be copied, reproduced, stored, sold, distributed, scanned, saved in any form of digital format or transmitted in any form digitally, without the written permission of the Publisher.

ISBN 9780860540403 paperback
ISBN 9781407348230 e-book
DOI https://doi.org/10.30861/9780860540403
A catalogue record for this book is available from the British Library
This book is available at www.barpublishing.com

CONTENTS

		Page
List of Figures		iii
Abbreviations		vii
Introduction		1

CHAPTER

I	Small Farmsteads	5
II	Farm and House	18
III	Rural Villas	29
IV	Slavery and Farms	40
V	Press-Rooms	49
VI	Granaries, Store-Rooms and Cattle-Sheds	57
VII	Chronology	63
Appendix A	An alphabetical catalogue of farm buildings discussed in the text	67
Appendix B	Other Sites	73
Bibliography		76

LIST OF FIGURES, MAPS AND PLATES

Figure		Page
1	A. Monte Forco. B. Enclosure farm near Luceria. C. Naxos I.	4
2	A. Posta Crusta. B. Sambuco. C. South Villa, Olynthus.	7
3	A. Selvasecca. B. 'Villa of Good Fortune', Olynthus. C. Tolve—Moltone.	8
4	A. Posto. B. Boscoreale Stazione.	13
5	A. Boscoreale Pisanella. B. Boscoreale Giuliana.;	19
6	Camerelle	23
7	A. Portaccia. B. Villa of Publius Fannius Sinistor.	25
8	San Rocco	30
9	Russi	32
10	Villa Magna	35
11	Cugno dei Vagni	36
12	A. Villa of Tiberius Claudius Eutychus. B. Gragnano.	41
13	A. Boscoreale Giuliana. B. Vicovaro.	44
14	Press-rooms	51
15	Store-rooms. Cattle-sheds.	58
Map I	Map showing the location of the farm buildings listed in Appendix A.	66
Map II	Map showing the location of the listed farm buildings in the region of Vesuvius.	72
Plate I	A. Wall painting from the House of the Small Fountain at Pompeii. B. Wall painting from the Villa of Publius Fannius Sinistor at Boscoreale.	39

ACKNOWLEDGEMENTS

In the preparation of this study I have received help and encouragement from a number of people to whom I should like to express my sincere thanks; Dr. R. J. Buck and Dr. R. C. Smith of the Department of Classics, The University of Alberta; Dr. D. G. Steele of the Department of Anthropology, The University of Alberta; and in particular Dr. A. M. Small, Director designate of The Canadian Academic Centre at Rome, whose recent excavations of Roman farm buildings in Southern Italy provided the initial stimulus for this study. For permission to reproduce the plates I should like to thank the following; The Oxford University Press (Plate 1a) and The Metropolitan Museum of Art, New York (Plate 1b). The figures have been redrawn by the author from previously published plans in order to establish a uniform scale throughout.

ABBREVIATIONS

Boethius and Ward-Perkins ERA — A. Boethius and J. B. Ward-Perkins, *Etruscan and Roman Architecture*, Harmondsworth, 1969.

Carrington 1931 — R. C. Carrington, 'Studies in the Campanian Villae Rusticae', *J.R.S.* XXI (1931), pp. 110-30.

1934 — Idem, 'Some ancient Italian country houses', *Antiquity* VIII (1934), pp. 261-280.

Cato DA — Marcus Porcius Cato, *De Agricultura*. Ed. by R. Goujard, Paris: Les Belles Lettres, 1975.

Columella DRR — L. Junius Moderatus Columella, *De Re Rustica*, Ed. by H. B. Ash, Cam. Mass.: Loeb Classical library, 1941.

Crova Edilizia — B. Crova, *Edilizia e tecnica rurale di Roma antica*. Milan: Fratelli Bocca, 1942.

Drachmann AOMP — A. G. Drachmann, *Ancient Oil Mills and Presses*. Copenhagen, 1932.

Frank ESAR — T. Frank, *An economic survey of ancient Rome*. Baltimore: Johns Hopkins University Press. 1933-40. 1959.

Palladius Op.Ag. — Rutilius Taurus Palladius, *Opus Agriculturae*. Ed. by R. H. Rodgers, Leipzig: Teubner, 1975.

Rickman Granaries — G. Rickman, *Roman granaries and storebuildings*. Cambridge University Press, 1971.

Rostovtzeff SEHRE — M. Rostovtzeff, *A social and economic history of the Roman empire*. 2nd ed., revised by P. M. Fraser, Oxford University Press 1957.

Varro RR — Marcus Terentius Varro, *Rerum Rusticarum libri III*. Ed. by H. B. Ash. Loeb Classical Library, 1934.

Vitruvius DA — Vitruvius Pollio, *De Architectura*. Ed. by F. Granger. New York: Loeb Classical Library, 1931.

White RF   K. D. White, Roman Farming. London: Thames and Hudson, 1970.

White FERW   Idem, Farm equipment of the Roman world. Cambridge University Press, 1975.

PERIODICALS

AJA	American Journal of Archaeology.
AMSMG	Atti e Memorie della Società Magna Grecia.
Bonn.Jahr.	Bonner Jahrbücher.
BSA	Annual of the British School at Athens.
CIL	Corpus Inscriptionum Latinarum.
JRS	Journal of Roman Studies.
MA	Monumenti Antichi.
MAAR	Memoirs of the American Academy at Rome.
MEFR	Melanges d'archéologie et d'histoire (Ecole Française de Rome).
NSc	Notizie degli Scavi.
PBSR	Papers of the British School at Rome.
PP	La Parola del Passato.
Rend.Linc.	Rendiconti dell'Accademia Nazionale dei Lincei.
Rev. Arch.	Revue Archéologique.
RPAA	Rendiconti della Pontifica Accademia Romana di Archeologia.
Röm. Mitth.	Mittheilungen des deutschen archeologischen Instituts Römische Abteilungen.

The following symbols have been used in the building plans to denote different pavement materials:

 Opus signinum. A waterproof concrete made with an agglomerate of crushed brick or stone.

 Opus spicatum. A paving of bricks laid in a herring-bone pattern.

 Mosaic.

 Marble slabs.

INTRODUCTION

The study of Roman farm buildings in Italy is one which, like other aspects of antiquity, has gone in and out of fashion. To a large extent this pattern of interest has reflected the ebb and flow of a more general interest in Pompeiana since, until relatively recently, most of our knowledge of Roman farms in Italy was derived from a small group of excavated sites in the region south and east of Vesuvius, the so-called 'Campanian villae rusticae'. Towards the end of the nineteenth century, accompanying a flurry of archaeological activity in and around Pompeii, several important works appeared in print, which described the excavations of a number of Roman farmhouses in this region. Foremost amongst these works was the volume by M. Ruggiero, Degli scavi di Stabia dal 1749 al 1782 (Naples, 1881). Also of great importance was a report of the now well-known farmhouse found at Boscoreale: A. Pasqui, 'La Villa Pompeiana della Pisanella presso Boscoreale', M.A. VII (1897). The excavations, often only partial, which were undertaken around the turn of the century of many other Campanian farms were not, however, published until the 1920s when M. Della Corte produced a long series of articles dealing with these farms. Unfortunately much desirable detail, in particular on points of construction materials, is lacking from these reports.

By the late 1920s about forty of the Campanian farms had been published and it was then that English-speaking scholars first began to take an interest in them. The first was Rostovtzeff who discussed the farms in his Social and Economic History of the Roman Empire (Oxford, 1926). This was followed by various articles dealing specifically with the Campanian farms, most notably R. C. Carrington's 'Studies in the Campanian villae rusticae', J.R.S. XXI (1931) and J. Day's 'Agriculture in the life of Pompeii', Yale Classical Studies III (1932). Later, after a lapse of some years, another important work appeared in Italian; this was a monograph by Bice Crova entitled Edilizia e tecnica rurale di Roma antica (Milan, 1942), which provided a comparative analysis of nearly all the Campanian farms and included discussion of different kinds of agricultural facilities.

In north Italy a number of rural villas were unearthed in the early part of the nineteenth century and their plans, often no more than the barest outlines, were published by M. Della Torre in Album dei disegni (Museo Cividale), 1827. These buildings have more recently been reconsidered by G. A. Mansuelli in the light of the valuable evidence that has been acquired from the excavations at the large rural villa at Russi in Emilia-Romagna; G. A. Mansuelli, 'La villa romana nell'Italia settentrionale', P.P. LVII (1957) and idem, Urbanistica e architettura della Cisalpina romana, Brussels 1971.

Other recent studies of farm buildings in Italy have included a monograph by J. E. Skydsgaard, Den Romerske Villa Rustica (Copenhagen, 1961) and chapters in K. D. White's Roman Farming (London, 1970) and J. Percival's

The Roman Villa (London, 1977). While these studies have appreciated the need to extend the field of research beyond the Campanian farms, they have tended to rely heavily on the traditional archaeological evidence and to reproduce the kind of analysis initiated by Rostovtzeff. Both Rostovtzeff and his immediate successors attempted to classify the Campanian farms into neatly packaged categories; a pressure to which the farms, with their immense variety of designs, do not comfortably submit. Only rarely is it possible to mark out a group of buildings which have a distinctive common characteristic. For example in chapter IV of this study I have grouped together a number of buildings which are distinguishable by a common architectural feature, in this case the existence of slave cells. In the first three chapters, however, the divisions that have been imposed are based on the simple criterion of scale. Farms are dealt with more or less according to size. Chapters V and VI deal with different kinds of farm facility which have been found in excavated farm buildings.

I have tried to concentrate mainly on the more recent archaeological evidence for farm buildings, since it is in this respect particularly that other studies have failed to keep pace with the ever increasing quantity of material. Thus of the forty or so farm buildings discussed here about half have been excavated within the last twenty-five years. Only twelve derive from the corpus of Campanian villae rusticae which has formed the basis for nearly every previous study of Roman farm buildings. I have tried to consider the archaeological evidence from every part of Italy and have if anything emphasised the non-Campanian material in an attempt to counter the bias which this has created in Italian villa studies.

Standards of excavation and publication have of course changed considerably since the early part of the century. The scope of investigation has become far more comprehensive. Thus, whereas an early report of the excavation of a farm building may provide little more than a plan of the building— often with no attempt to distinguish building phases—and perhaps some information on the objects retrieved from the various rooms, a modern excavation will aim to provide information not only on the form and date of the structures encountered, but also an analysis of all the finds including those, such as bones and seeds, which will help to reconstruct the agricultural economy of the farm. The term "villa studies" now covers a broad area of research, including not only primary analysis of excavated material but consideration of a site in its broader economic and social context.

The present study, however, is restricted to a consideration of the architecture, and specifically the lay-out, of Roman farm buildings and their various facilities. A glance at any of the major works on Roman architecture will show how neglected has been the study of Roman rural architecture. Over the years farm buildings have been unearthed in almost every region of Italy but the reports of these excavations have remained scattered and sadly neglected. The main difficulty facing a study of this kind is the varying nature of these reports. Inevitably as excavation techniques have become more scientific, the reports have become more comprehensive. Yet even from the earlier and less detailed reports something of value can generally be extracted on the question of design. Thus it has been possible to attempt a comparative study of farm architecture, making use of excavation reports published throughout the last one hundred years.

Finally a word must be said concerning terminology. By convention the term "villa rustica" has often been used to refer to a Roman farm building. This is strictly incorrect since the term is used by the Roman agronomists to refer only to that part of the farm which was used purely for agricultural functions. The word "villa" on the other hand, as J. Harmand ('Sur le valeur archéologique du mot "villa" ', Rev. Arch. 37 (1970), pp. 155-8) has pointed out was used fairly freely in antiquity to refer to any rural building (or even the land it occupied) much as the word "farm" is used today. In English the word "villa" has, I think, certain connotations which make it inapplicable to most farm buildings, except perhaps those built on a grand scale and incorporating lavish residential facilities. Thus I have used the word "villa" to refer to the large building complexes discussed in chapter III. Elsewhere I have preferred to use the English word "farm" and its compound forms "farmstead", to refer to the smaller farm buildings, and "farmhouse" where agricultural and residential facilities are integrated in a compact single structure.

FIG 1

A Monte Forco

B Enclosure farm near Luceria

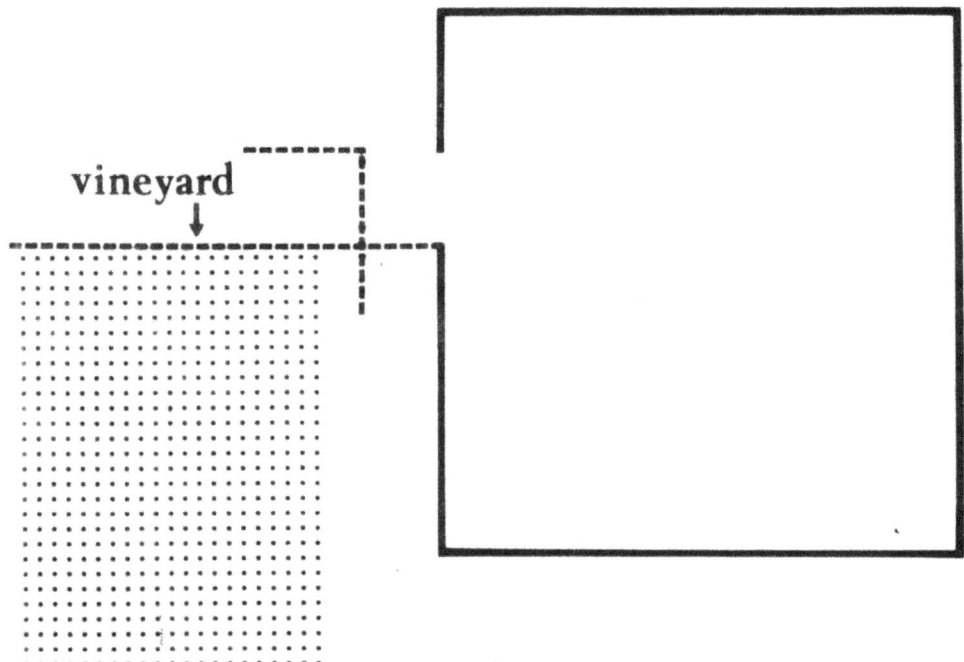

C Naxos 1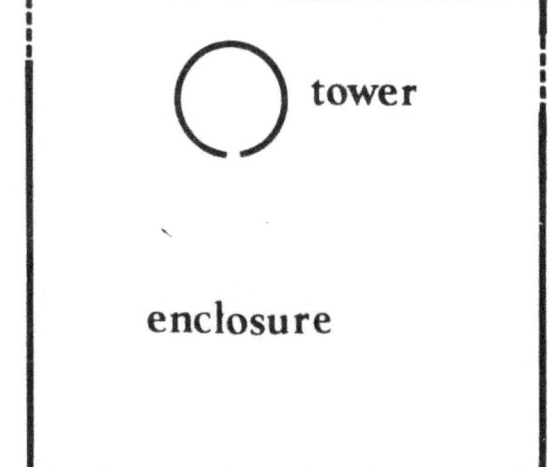

scale 1:500

CHAPTER I

SMALL FARMSTEADS

Although an increasing number of small farm sites have been identified from topographical surveys in various parts of Italy, very few of these sites have been systematically excavated.[1] For a knowledge of the architecture of the small farms of Roman Italy one has, therefore, to depend on information from a limited number of farm sites, which may be representative of a more general pattern. The farmhouses discussed in this chapter are all of an unsophisticated character, though they vary considerably in their architectural form. The size and quality of the buildings no doubt reflect the economic return of the farms and, accordingly, the area of the land holdings associated with them. We do not yet know nearly enough about the role that the small farm played in the pattern of land use, particularly to what extent it survived alongside the larger farm units of the Catonian type. There is, therefore, much need for the careful study and dating of small farmstead sites to help reconstruct the ancient landscape.

A very simple type of farmhouse is probably represented by the excavated site on Monte Forco in the Ager Capenas (Cat. 18. Fig. 1a). Here were found the remains of a rectangular structure (10.95 x 5.10 m), built in opus reticulatum with tufa quoins, which appears to date in origin to the late 1st century B.C. By its relation to neighbouring sites, it seems to have been the farm building of a small-holding of around five or six iugera, and it has been suggested by the excavator that this holding may have been connected with the land distributions to Caesar's veterans after 46 B.C.[2] The building had a simple rectangular plan, but its restoration in elevation must remain uncertain. The thickness of the walls (0.47 m) does not rule out the possibility that the building was of two storeys.[3] The evidence of wall-paintings suggests that simple two-storeyed farm buildings were a common feature of the Roman landscape,[4] as for example in the well-known wall-painting from the house of the 'Small Fountain' in Pompeii (Plate 1a), which depicts a rural scene with two apparently rectangular tower-like structures.[5] In both these buildings it appears that only the upper storeys have windows, which suggests that the ground floors were used for purely agricultural purposes, such as the storage of farm tools or the stalling of barnyard animals. The upper floors may have served as storage lofts or else have contained modest living quarters. The building in the foreground of the painting has what appears to be a wooden balcony at first floor level; access to the upper storey may therefore have been by means of an external ladder.[6]

A rudimentary type of two-storeyed tower may also have existed within some of the farm enclosures detected by aerial photography in the centuriated landscape north-east of Luceria in Apulia.[7] If this could be shown by excavation, one might witness here in south Italy an arrangement of tower and enclosure which would echo the simple scheme of compound and tower, which J. H. Young has identified as a common feature of the countryside of Greece "between the late sixth and (earlier?) third centuries B.C."[8] The size of the enclosure seen in Plate IIIB of Bradford's article (reproduced here as a line drawing, Fig. 1b) is approximately 36 metres square. This compares favourably with Young's Naxos I enclosure which measures 35 x 32 metres (Fig. 1c). This contained a single circular tower structure about 8.5 m in diameter. The enclosures were presumably designed to act as folds for livestock, for which the six foot ditch of the Roman example, probably reinforced by fencing, would have served adequately. Many of the farms of the ager centuriatus of Luceria, most of which is dated to the 2nd century B.C., were apparently ten iugera in size, though some earlier allotments may not have greatly exceeded the traditional two iugera plot, which represented the division of the centuria of 200 iugera into one hundred equal allotments.[9] The farm illustrated seems to have functioned on a mixed economy; in addition to keeping livestock, the farmer was doubtless responsible for the cultivation of the adjacent vineyard. The type of small farm unit seen here in the centuriated landscape near Luceria may have been a feature of other centuriated areas in Italy though more evidence would be required to substantiate this.

Another kind of small farmstead is represented in Italy by two buildings which, although found in different regions and dating from different centuries, have a strikingly similar design. One is the Villa Sambuco excavated near Blera in southern Etruria and dating from the 2nd century B.C. (Cat. 26.Fig. 2b); the other a recently excavated building at Posta Crusta near Ordona in Apulia (Cat. 22. Fig. 2a), which, in its phase II form, which interests us here, has been dated to the early Empire. In both these buildings the arrangement of the rooms is similar. A central corridor, extending almost the complete length of the building, separates ranges of rooms to the north and south.

At the Villa Sambuco the northern rooms (rooms 1-4 on the plan) appear to have been store rooms while those to the south were for domestic use.[10] The proposed restoration of a tower for room 10 seems doubtful, given the room's limited dimensions (only 1.22 mm in width). Could a tower as narrow as this have served a useful function "for defence"? The suggestion of a second storey over part of the house seems more likely.[11]

The building at Posta Crusta presents a very close parallel in its plan. With the exception of room 8, which served as a modest tablinum, the rooms to the north of the central corridor (2 on the plan) were used for agricultural purposes. They included facilities for the processing of olive oil (rooms 9, 10, 11). The rooms to the south of the corridor formed the domestic part of the house.[12] The dimensions of the two farmsteads correspond closely (see below, p. 10). Whether or not the central corridor of either building was enclosed under a pitched roof is not certain. De Boe points out the difficulties of lighting that would have resulted had this been the case at the Posta Crusta farm. Ostenberg, however, proposes a single roof over the whole building for the Villa Sambuco.[13] It seems likely in both cases that the corridor space was at least partially open to the sky and formed a small internal courtyard. Even if the end rooms were roofed the area of the courtyard would still have been around 40 square metres. Courtyards smaller than this are known from other sites.[14]

FIG 2

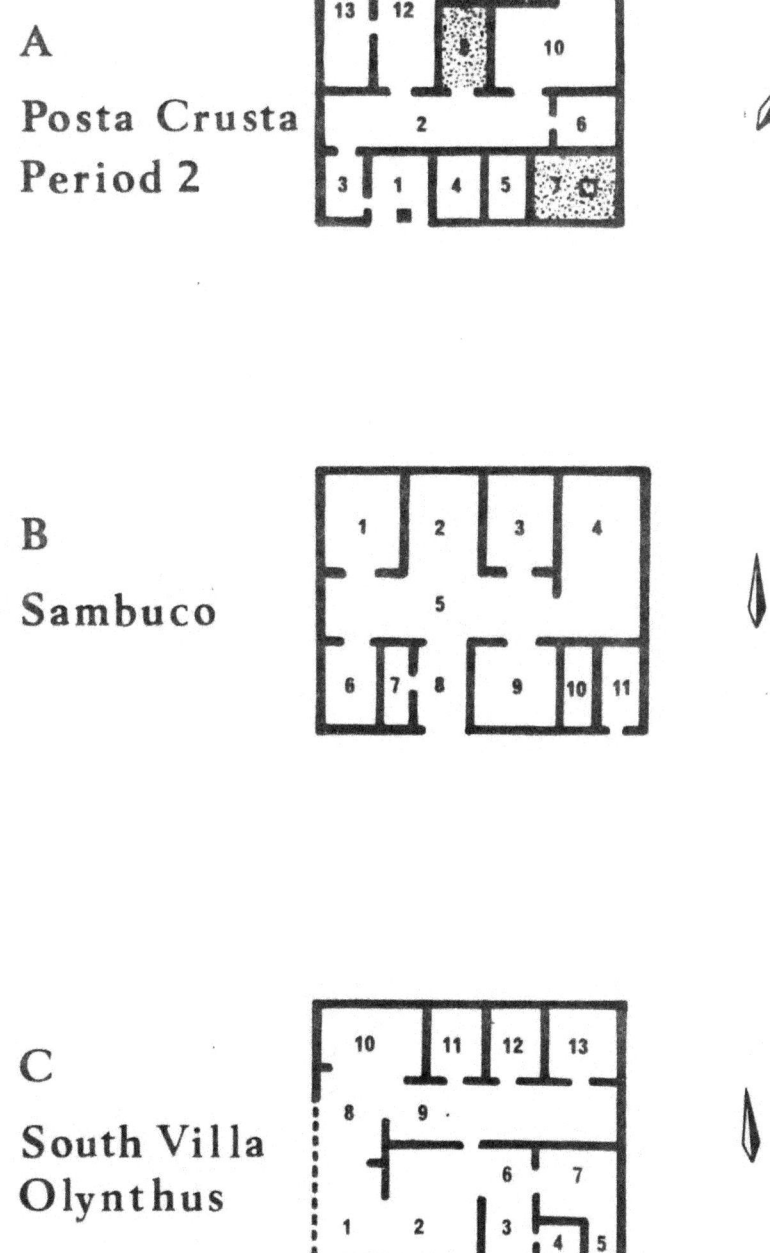

A
Posta Crusta
Period 2

B
Sambuco

C
South Villa
Olynthus

FIG 3

A
Selvasecca

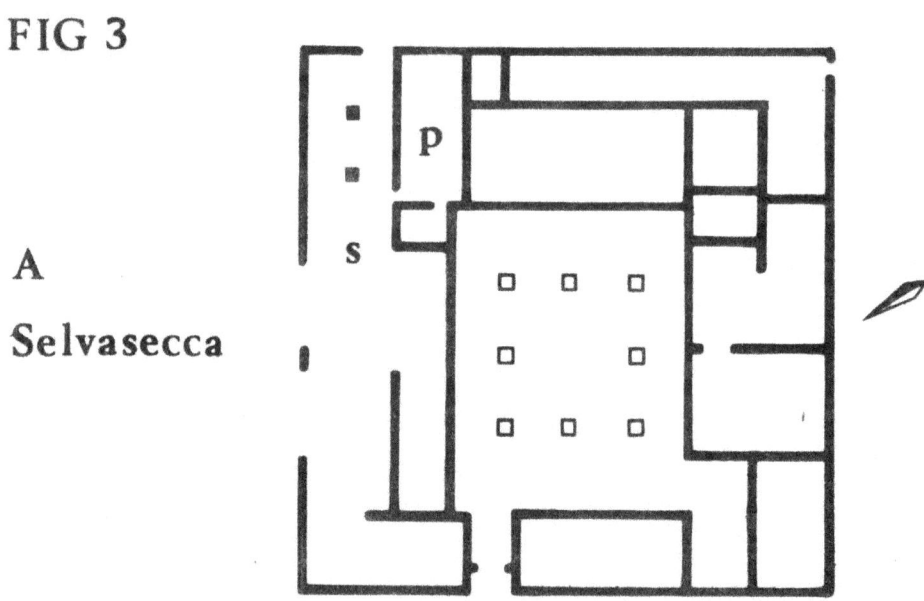

B
Villa of Good Fortune
Olynthus

C
Tolve
Moltone

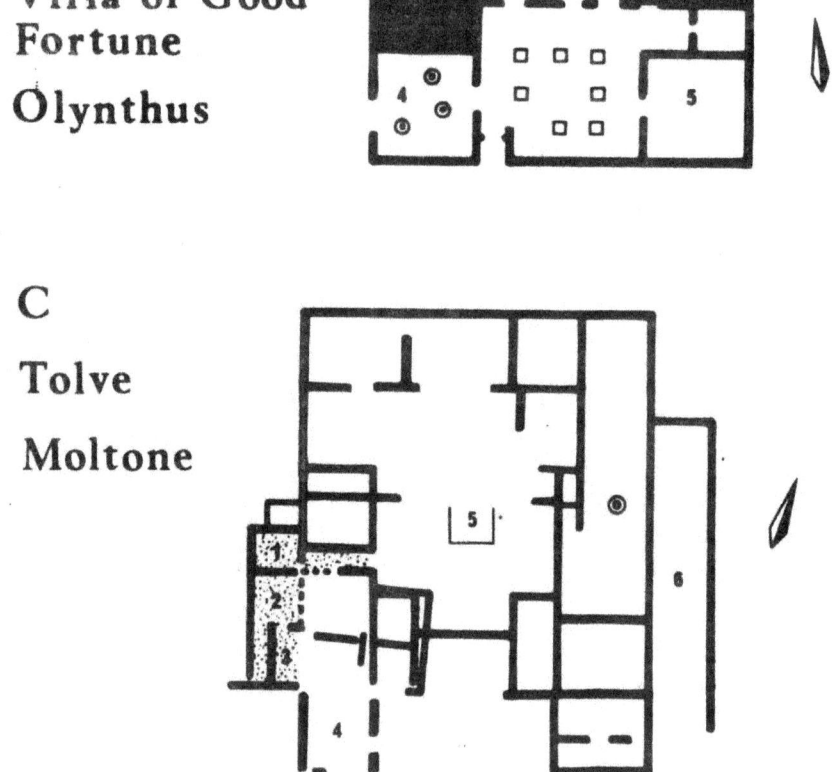

Fig. 2a. Posta Crusta (after De Boe). Scale 1:500.
Period 2.

    1. Entrance hallway
    2. Corridor (? court)
    3-7. Domestic rooms
    8. Tablinum
    9. Press-room
    10. Store-room
    11. ? Milling room
    12-13. Uncertain use

Fig. 2b. Sambuco (after Ostenberg). Scale 1:500.

    1-4. Store-rooms
    5. Corridor (? court)
    6. ? Stable
    7. Stairwell
    8. Entrance hallway
    9. ? Kitchen
    10. (? tower)
    11. Store shed

Fig. 2c. South Villa, Olynthus (after Robinson). Scale 1:500.

    1. Uncertain use
    2/6. Courtyard
    3. Front hall (? shop)
    4. Kitchen
    5. Bathroom
    7. Oecus
    8. Uncertain use
    9. παστάς
    10-13. Domestic rooms

Fig. 3a. Selvasecca (after Berggren). Scale 1:500.

    p. ? Press-room
    s. Store-room/barn

Fig. 3b. Villa of Good Fortune, Olynthus (after Robinson and Graham).
Scale 1:500.

    1. Andron
    2. Kitchen
    3. Guest room
    4. Store-room
    5. Domestic rooms

Fig. 3c. Tolve-Moltone (after Tocca). Scale 1:500.

    1-3. Bath rooms
    4. ? Tower
    5. Impluvium
    6. Livestock pen

The construction materials employed at the two farmsteads were different, no doubt reflecting the relative availability of good building stone. At the Villa Sambuco the wall socles were constructed with squared blocks of tufa, locally quarried. These supported a superstructure of plastered mud-brick and a tiled roof. At Posta Crusta the socles for the mud-brick walls were constructed with mortared river stones and rubble. The width of the walls, c. 0.50 m at each site, indicates the load-bearing potential for a second storey but there is no clear indication that such existed in either case.

The similarity in design of the Villa Sambuco and the Posta Crusta farmstead is such as to suggest a common architectural source for both. That two buildings in different parts of Italy, apparently belonging to quite different periods, should bear such a striking resemblance to one another cannot be coincidental. The source for their design is surely to be found in the domestic architecture of the Greek world. It must be remembered that many Greek town houses in fact functioned as farm buildings in conditions where the countryside was farmed from the towns. In the internal corridor of the Italian farmsteads there would seem to be a reflection of the Greek παστάς, an internal cross-hall extending across the house in front of the northern range of rooms, which is found commonly in Greek house plans.[15] A particularly close parallel can be seen between the design of the Italian farms and that of the South Villa at Olynthus.[16] The excavators of this house comment on the uncommon absence of an internal court which, according to the usual Olynthian house type, normally existed to the south of the παστάς. This absence, however, may indicate that the central corridor in fact served in place of the usual court, as an open space for keeping barnyard animals and farm equipment. The relative dimensions of house and corridor of the South Villa at Olynthus correspond closely to those of the Italian farmsteads as follows (measurements in metres):

	House	Corridor
South Villa	21.1 x 17.0	14.8 x 3.1
Villa Sambuco	22.6 x 17.3	15.0 x 3.8
Posta Crusta	20.8 x 19.2	15.7 x 3.5

Another farmstead found in the region of Blera is the so-called Villa Selvasecca (Cat. 33. Fig. 3a). Although a slightly more elaborate structure than the two farmsteads discussed above, this was a building of modest proportions and an essentially simple layout. The plan of the farmstead was in the form of a square (36.0 x 35.5 m) with rooms arranged around a central peristyle. The architecture of the building and the materials of construction reveal the owner's intention of providing himself with a house which was both a functional farm building and a comfortable, though not opulent, dwelling. The peristyle and court were constructed with care and the materials employed—the squared tufa paving stones of the court and the stone columns and capitals of the colonnade—suggest that the court was not used for agricultural purposes. Most of the agricultural activity within the farmhouse seems to have been concentrated in the northern and eastern wings. The long outer room on the north side of the building was probably a barn or stable, having access directly to the outside through one large or two small separate doorways.[17] The discovery at the Villa Selvasecca of a workshop for the manufacturing of roof tiles revealed one aspect of the farmstead's economy. This at any rate was the interpretation given by the excavator of the various stone-cut basins and moulds found in the rooms on the north side of the house.[18] Other finds from these rooms included fragments of dolia and amphorae and the bases of presses. The south-west corner of the building contained the rooms for domestic use. Here traces of painted wall-plaster and of white mosaic indicated that the residential part of the farmstead did not lack interior decoration, although it is possible that some of the decorative features were added after the original occupation of the house in the mid-2nd century B.C. The farm's life extended into the early Imperial period and the domestic quarters are unlikely to have escaped redecoration. The construction of the wall socles was similar to that at the Villa Sambuco, using blocks of locally quarried tufa. At the Villa Selvasecca, however, it appears that the mud-brick superstructure was held in a framework of timber. A series of holes was drilled at intervals into the flat upper surface of the tufa socle in order to secure the timbers, a building technique which is found in buildings in Etruria at an earlier period.[19] The walls could have supported an upper storey though again it is uncertain whether such existed or not. The roof was tiled, using terracotta tegulae and imbrices evidently produced at the site.[20]

It is to Olynthus too that we should look for the type of building which provides the model for the architecture of the Villa Selvasecca. A number of the houses found at Olynthus contained in their plan a complete internal peristyle.[21] One of these, the so-called "Villa of Good Fortune" (Fig. 3b), presents a marked similarity in plan to the Villa Selvasecca. In each case the peristyle is placed more or less centrally, only nearer to that side of the house on which the main entrance lies. The entrance is similarly sited and designed in both houses. The doorway is set back from the front wall of the house, creating a small porch (πρόθυρον) in front of the door. Also similar is the treatment of the courtyard flooring, in that the central and exposed area of the peristyle is given a paving which stops at the line of the colonnade and does not extend beneath the surrounding porticos.[22]

A partial parallel can also be seen between the architecture of the Villa Selvasecca and that of a recently discovered small Hellenistic farmhouse at Tolve in Basilicata (Cat. 36.Fig. 3c). The Tolve farmhouse was similarly designed in the form of a square around an internal courtyard, which in this case had a central brick-paved impluvium, supplied by means of an aqueduct from a nearby spring. The main entrance lay to the south but, unlike that of the Villa Selvasecca, it was sited centrally. An interesting architectural feature of the building is the two projecting rooms which flank the main entrance. The increased thickness of the walls of the room which projects to the west of the entrance (Fig. 3c, 4) suggests that it may have supported a greater load and that there may therefore have been a tower attached to the farmhouse at this point. That such towers were often incorporated into Greek farmhouses is well attested from archaeological, literary and epigraphic evidence.[23] Moreover this structural feature also appears in several Greek colonial farmhouses, including one at Cassamassima al Campagnolo in Basilicata, within the chora of the Greek city of Metapontum.[24]

To the south-west of the courtyard was a suite of bath rooms (Fig. 3c, 1,2,3) with plastered walls and opus signinum floors. Traces of painted plaster indicated that the rooms to the north and west of the courtyard were probably for domestic use, while those to the east, where finds included pieces of iron tools and part of a loom, were apparently used for the agricultural and industrial functions of the farmstead.[25] To the very east of the building was an open-ended enclosure (Fig. 3c,6) which may have served for penning livestock. A nearby kiln evidently produced the tiles and various terracotta mouldings used in the construction of the house.[26]

More evidence for the architecture of the small farm comes from Campania. Of the many farms that have been excavated in this region, two in particular stand out by virtue of their relative simplicity and the essentially "rustic" character of their design and construction. One of these is the Posto Villa at Francolise (Cat. 23. Fig. 4a), which in its earliest phase dates to the end of the 2nd century B.C. At this time, the building had an unpretentious and highly functional aspect. The lay-out was in the form of a large open courtyard, round which were ranged, on three sides at any rate, the farm buildings. On the west side of the yard stood a roofed portico, which perhaps served as a stable for cattle or other animals. That the farm's economy was in part based on the rearing of livestock is suggested by the size of the yard (532 m^2 approx.), in which herds or flocks could easily be penned. The living quarters of the farm were apparently along the north side of the yard, where the remains of two rooms with opus signinum floors were found. Here some indication is given of how the building was constructed in elevation. Above a socle of squared tufa blocks the walls were made of limestone rubble packed into a timber framework (opus craticium), a technique somewhat similar to that used in the Villa Selvasecca (above, p.11). The lay-out of the Posto farm bears some relation to the type of "enclosure farm" which we have encountered in Apulia and which, I have suggested, may derive from the "enclosure-and-tower" arrangement found in numerous Greek farms. In the Posto farm we find not a tower-like structure, but a range of rooms used for different agricultural and domestic purposes. Rather than a building within an enclosure, we see the enclosure and building incorporated into an integrated unit. The farm remained in its original form for about fifty years, but around the middle of the 1st century B.C., it was reconstructed and enlarged, probably indicating a change of ownership. Perhaps the capacity of the farm had to be increased to meet the requirements of a larger land holding.

An equally unpretentious farmhouse is that excavated in 1903 near the railway station at Boscoreale near Pompeii (Cat. 4. Fig. 4b). The rooms of this building were simply constructed with plain plastered walls and trodden earth floors.[27] The farmhouse was designed primarily as a functional unit and incorporated only modest living quarters. Most of the rooms were evidently used for the production or storage of agricultural produce. It is interesting to observe that the largest room in the farmhouse is the kitchen (No. 12 on the plan). This recalls Varro's claim that in the old-fashioned and simple type of farmhouse, a good kitchen was a primary feature.[28] It serves too to illustrate Mau's idea that the atrium, which became the principal room of the Roman town house, had its counterpart in the farmhouse kitchen with its central hearth. When, in an urban context, the atrium lost its central

FIG 4

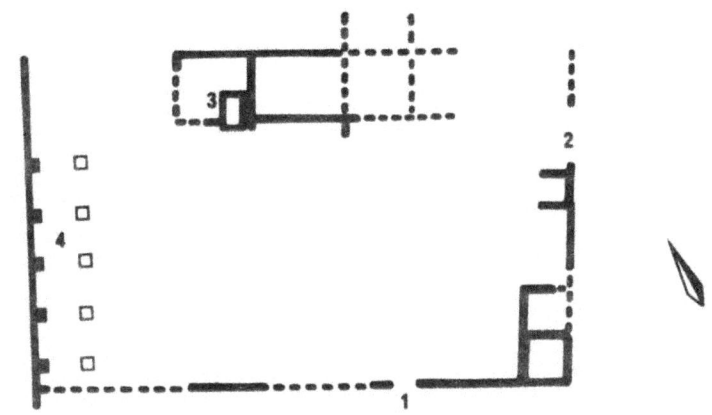

A

Posto Period I (after Von Blankenhagen, Cotton and Ward-Perkins)
Scale 1:500.

1/2 Entrances to courtyard
3   Settling tank
4   Cattle stalls

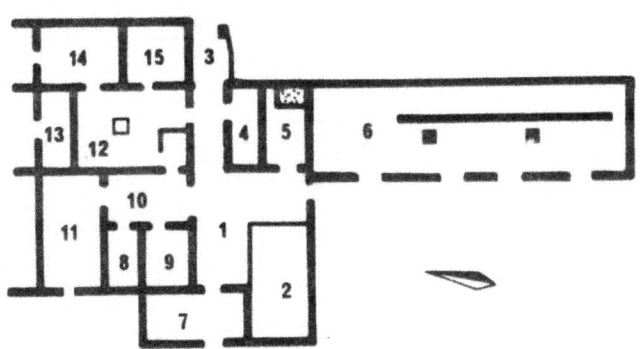

B

Boscoreale Stazione (after Della Corte). Scale 1:500.

1	Courtyard	11	Store-room
2	Garden	12	Kitchen
3	Main entrance	13	Uncertain use
4	Domestic room	14	Sheep fold
5	Press-room	15	Triclinium
6	Storage barn		
7	Store-room		
8-10	Domestic rooms		

hearth, it also lost its original function. The kitchen in the town-house never regained its importance, but was arbitrarily accommodated.[29]

Storage facilities were spread throughout the farm. No doubt use was made of the long barn (No. 6) for this purpose, as well as rooms 7 ("tettoia con dolia") and 11 (horreum). All these rooms had direct access to the outside, on that side of the farmhouse which faced the country.[30] This would mean that carts could load and unload right at the door of the store-rooms.

The excavation showed signs of a mixed farm economy. In room 2 were found the remains of a small wine-press. Such presses could not have been cheap in antiquity, and a privately-owned press such as this one suggests that the owner of the farm must have had reasonable returns from the sale of his wine, some of which was apparently sold on the premises (reducing transportation costs). In addition to producing wine, the farm reared sheep and chickens, while the long barn may have been used for stabling larger herds of livestock.[31] The location of the sheep-pen next to the kitchen (Fig. 4b.14) recalls Vitruvius' and Varro's instructions that the warmest part of the house, that part nearest to the kitchen, should be used to stable livestock (both authors recommend cows, however).[32]

The date of the Boscoreale Stazione farm was not scientifically established by the excavator. The plan appears to be of an integrated structure, and suggests a single building phase. Della Corte describes the building as "very similar" to another farmhouse in the same region (Cat. 2), which was constructed in opus incertum, and it is possible that this similarity included a likeness in building technique.[33] If so, the farmhouse may date from the early part of the 1st century B.C., perhaps from the period following the establishment of the Sullan colony in 80 B.C.

A number of the small farmsteads discussed in this chapter have been dated to the 2nd century B.C. (Cat. 23, 26, 33). Several others were constructed in the 1st century B.C. (Cat. 4, 18, ?22). Occupation, however, of most of the buildings, apparently without any major architectural modifications, seems to have continued in the 1st century A.D. (Cat. 4, 18, 22, 26, 33). Further reconstruction and enlargement of the original buildings is attested at only two of the sites (Cat. 22, 23). The buildings are of course few in number and provide insufficient evidence to draw any firm conclusions about the role of the small farmstead in the developing pattern of land tenure. The evidence they provide, however, does suggest that under the early Empire, although the growth of larger estates may have affected the status of some smallholders, this process did not necessarily bring about a decline in the occupation of small farmstead sites in Italy.

The architecture of the buildings discussed varies considerably. We have observed the apparent influence of Greek domestic architecture in the design of a number of the Roman farmsteads (Cat. 22, 26, 33) and have also suggested a possible link between the kind of farm compounds detected in Apulia and at Francolise and the type of "enclosure farm" known in Greece. The Greek colonial farmsteads which are now being increasingly studied in South Italy may provide some evidence for the means whereby these patterns of Greek farmhouse architecture first found their way into the Italian peninsula.[34] While making use of these imported traditions, a regional character was given to the Roman farmsteads by the variety of the available materials used in their construction.

NOTES

1. The major work in Italian is the series of topographical studies published by the Istituto di Topografia Antica dell'Università di Roma, under the title Forma Italiae. In English the pioneering studies by John Bradford Remain of great value, though the results of related field work have yet to be published; J. Bradford, Ancient Landscapes, London 1957; idem, 'Siticulosa Apulia', Antiquity XX (1946), pp. 191-200; idem, 'Buried landscapes in southern Italy', Antiquity XXIII (1949), pp. 58-72; idem, 'The Apulian expedition: an interim report', Antiquity XXIV (1950), pp. 84-95. Other studies of rural settlement include: G. Duncan, 'Sutri-notes on southern Etruria—3', P.B.S.R. XIII (1958), pp. 63-134; G.D.B. Jones, 'Capena and the Ager Capenas' (2 parts), P.B.S.R. XVII (1962), pp. 116-207, XVIII (1963), pp. 100-158; A. Kahane, L. M. Threipland, J. B. Ward-Perkins, 'The Ager Veientanus, north and east of Rome', P.B.S.R. XXIII (1968); D. Scagliarini, Ravenna e le ville romane di Romagna (Coll. quaderni di antichità Ravennati, No. X), Ravenna 1968; P. Vinson, 'Ancient roads between Venosa and Gravina', P.B.S.R. XXVII (1972), pp. 58-90.

2. Jones, op.cit. (1963), p. 157.

3. For a discussion of the load-bearing abilities of mud-brick walls see J. E. Jones, A. J. Graham and L. H. Sackett, 'An Attic country house below the cave of Pan at Vari', B.S.A. 68 (1973), pp. 425-7, 438-40, where the authors point out that "a very common unit for the socles of mud-brick house walls was a width of 0.40-0.50 m, that is, one cubit or a foot and a half on almost any Greek standard; and Vitruvian precept (11.18.17) and modern examples suggest that this would support one upper floor, but no more".

4. For the evidence of wall-paintings see P. Grimal, 'Les maisons à tour Hellénistiques et Romaines', M.E.F.R. (1939), pp. 28-59. In particular section B—11e série, pp. 34-8; R. Ling, 'Studius and the beginnings of Roman landscape painting', J.R.S. LXXVII (1977), pp 1-16. The evidence from mosaics must be treated with caution. Most of it is provincial and much of it late. The African mosaics have been studied by T. Precheur-Canonge, La Vie Rurale en Afrique d'apres les mosaiques (Publications de l'Université de Tunis), Paris 1962, who suggests that most of the small structures that appear in landscape scenes are probably the dependent outbuildings, barns, granaries, dovecotes etc. of large villas. Such tower-like structures as appear on the Zliten mosaic (S. Aurigemma, Italy in Africa: archaeological discoveries 1911-1943. Vol. I. Part I., Rome 1960, Plate 125) have a distinctly North African character, which probably derives from the architecture of Hellenistic Egypt, and which manifests itself in late Roman Africa in the form of

the gasr, a type of fortified tower; S. Stucchi, Architettura Cirenaica, Rome 1975, pp. 518-20.

5. Rostoftzeff SEHRE, p. 65, Plate X.1; idem, 'Die hellenistisch-romische Architekturlandschaft', Röm.Mitth. XXVI (1911), p. 95, Plate XI.1; S. Reinach, Repertoire de peinture Grecque et Romaine, Paris 1922, p. 386, No. 2.

6. Compare the proposed reconstruction of the tower-like farm building at Köln-Mungersdorf; H. Hinz, 'Zur Bauweise der Villa rustica', Gymnasion VII (1970), p. 24.

7. Bradford, op.cit. (1949), pp. 58-72, especially Plates IIIA and B; E. T. Salmon, Roman colonisation under the Republic, London 1969, Plate 6; White R.F., Plate 12; A. H. McDonald, Republican Rome, London 1966, Plate 71.

8. J. H. Young, 'Studies in south Attica: country estates at Sounion', Hesperia XXV (1956), p. 142; cf. J. Pecirka, 'Homestead farms in classical and Hellenistic Hellas', in M. I. Finley, Problèmes de la terre en Grèce ancienne, Paris 1973, pp. 113-147.

9. A. Toynbee, Hannibal's Legacy. Vol. II, Oxford 1965, p. 563ff.; M. W. Frederiksen, 'The contribution of archaeology to the agrarian problem in the Gracchan period', Dialoghi di Archeologia II-III (1970-1), pp. 343-4. For the traditional 2 iugera plot, E. T. Salmon, op.cit., p. 168, note 21, with a list of ancient sources. For the subdivision of centuriae in general, O. A. W. Dilke, The Roman Land surveyors, Newton Abbot 1971, pp. 93-6.

10. C. Ostenberg, 'Luni and Villa Sambuco', in Etruscan culture, land and people, Malmo 1960, pp. 318-9.

11. Ibid., p. 319.

12. G. De Boe, 'Villa romana in località "Posta Crusta". Rapporto provisorio sulle campagne di scavo 1972 e 1973', N.Sc. 1975, p. 521.

13. Ibid., p. 521; Ostenberg, op.cit., p. 317.

14. For example in the Greek farm at Lago del Lupo in the chora of Metapontum, where the internal court measures approximately 8.3 x 4.5 m (37.4 m^2).

15. D. M. Robinson and J. W. Graham, Excavations at Olynthus, Part VIII: The Hellenic House, Baltimore 1938; J. W. Graham, 'Origins and inter-relations of the Greek house and the Roman house', Phoenix XX (Spring 1966), pp. 3-31.

16. D. M. Robinson, Excavations at Olynthus, Part XII: Domestic and Public Architecture, Baltimore 1948, pp. 259-63. Plate 222.

17. For comparative store-rooms and barns see below, Chapter VI.

18. E. Berggren and A. Andren, 'Blera (località Selvasecca)—villa rustica etrusco-romana con manifattura di terracotte architettoniche', N.Sc. 1969, pp. 55-6.

19. E. Berggren, 'A new approach to the closing centuries of Etruscan history', Arctos V (1967), p. 33; K. Hanell, 'San Giovenale: the Acropolis', in Etruscan culture, land and people, p. 301.

20. Berggren, op.cit., p. 36.

21. Robinson and Graham, op.cit., p. 160.

22. Contrast, for example, the courtyard paving of the Vari House; Jones, Graham and Sackett, op.cit., p. 433.

23. For a full discussion of the evidence, with bibliography, see Jones, Graham and Sackett, op.cit., p. 437, notes 230-34.

24. G. Uggeri, ' ΚΛΗΡΟΙ arcaici e bonifica classica nella ΧΩΡΑ di Metaponto', P.P. CXXIV (1969), p. 52. note 4.

25. G. Tocca, 'L'attività archeologica nella Basilicata settentrionale', in Atti del XIII convegno di studi sulla Magna Grecia, Napoli 1974, p. 462.

26. Ibid., p. 465.

27. Crova, Edilizia, p. 44.

28. Varro, R. R., I. XIII.2, I.XIII.6 ('illic laudabatur villa si habebat culinum rusticam bonam—in those days a farm was thought highly of if it had a good rustic kitchen'); cf. Columella, D.R.R., I. VI.3 ('at in rustica parte magna et alta culina ponetur—and in the agricultural part of the house there should be a large kitchen with a high ceiling').

29. A. Mau and F. W. Kelsey, Pompeii, its life and art, New York 1899, pp. 253-4, 266-8.

30. Crova, Edilizia, p. 43, Fig. 1 (A^1), calls the entrance into room 7 'ingresso verso la campagna'.

31. Sheep in rooms 10 and 11; Della Corte, N.Sc. 1921, p. 439; chickens according to a graffito found in the farmhouse (C.I.L. IV.6873); the existence of three doors into the barn suggests that it may have been divided internally with wooden fencing so that part of it could be used for stabling and part for storage.

32. Varro, R.R., I. XIII. I; Vitruvius, D.A., I. VI. I.

33. Della Corte, N.Sc. 1921, p. 436; ibid., pp. 423-6; Crova, Edilizia, p. 45, simply refers to the farm as 'Republican'.

34. Recent studies include D. Adamesteanu, 'Le suddivisione di terra nel Metapontino', in M. I. Finley, op.cit., pp. 49-61; G. Uggeri, op.cit., (note 24).

CHAPTER II

FARM AND HOUSE

Central to a study of farm buildings in Italy is the type of building which combines in an integrated structure the functional requirements of both a working farm and a fashionable residence. This type of farm building is well represented by excavated examples in Italy, though the lay-out of the different farms varies considerably, according to local tradition, personal taste and the type of agriculture practised. The combination of working farm and residence suggests that these farms were occupied by their owners for most of the year, if not permanently, and run as family concerns. The capital outlay on the agricultural facilities of the farms is matched by expenditure on the residential quarters. There can be little doubt that the owners of these farms were wealthy men, and it seems reasonable to suppose that their wealth, from wherever it may have derived, was maintained by the efficient running of their farms.

The locus classicus of this type of building is the famous farmhouse at Boscoreale Pisanella (Cat. 3. Fig. 5a). Excavated towards the end of the 19th century, the farmhouse has been frequently discussed, for example by Mau, Crova and White.[1] Attention has been focused on the arrangement and relationship of the different rooms of the farm, and on how this corresponds to the recommendations given by the various Roman writers who discuss farm buildings. Day has attempted to calculate the size of the farm on the basis of the storage facilities within the excavated building.[2] Only Crova has observed that the Boscoreale farmhouse is remarkably similar in design to another farmhouse excavated around the same time at Boscoreale (contrada Giuliana) (Cat. 1. Fig. 5b).[3] The similarity is unlikely to be coincidental, considering the proximity of the two farms, and one may suppose that either the one directly influenced the design of the other, or that both reflect a local tradition of farm design which may have been echoed in several farmhouses in the same region. It seems appropriate therefore to discuss these two farms together.

The central feature of each is an open court which, to some extent, separates the domestic and agricultural quarters of the farms. The former are ranged together behind a portico. In each case, the prominence of the kitchen is noticeable (Fig. 5a, 7; Fig. 5b, 9), recalling the precepts of Varro and Columella.[4] The other major room of the residential area is the triclinium (Fig. 5a, 3; Fig. 5b, 2). In both houses, the walls of this room were decorated with painted plaster. Many fragments of the paintings from the Villa Pisanella are now in the Field Museum of Natural History in Chicago.[5]

The rooms devoted to the needs of agriculture occupy the larger part of the farms. Largest of these in each case is the storage room for wine and oil (the cella vinaria or olearia: Fig. 5a, 21; Fig. 5b, 7). These contained

FIG 5

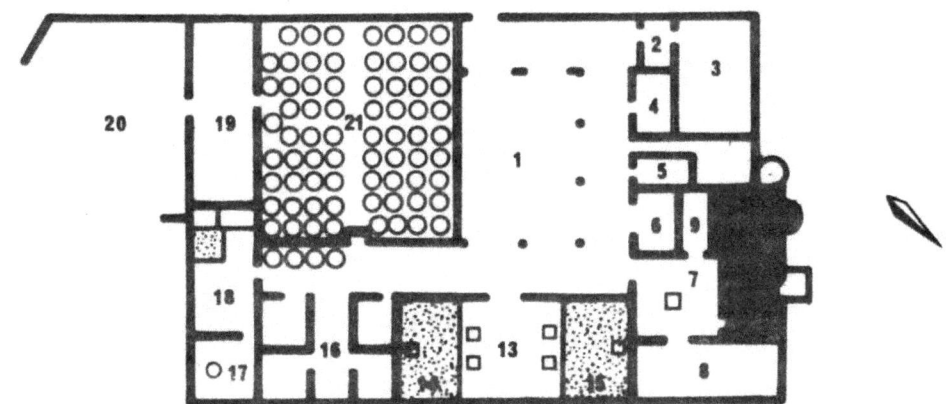

A

Boscoreale Pisanella

B

Boscoreale Giuliana

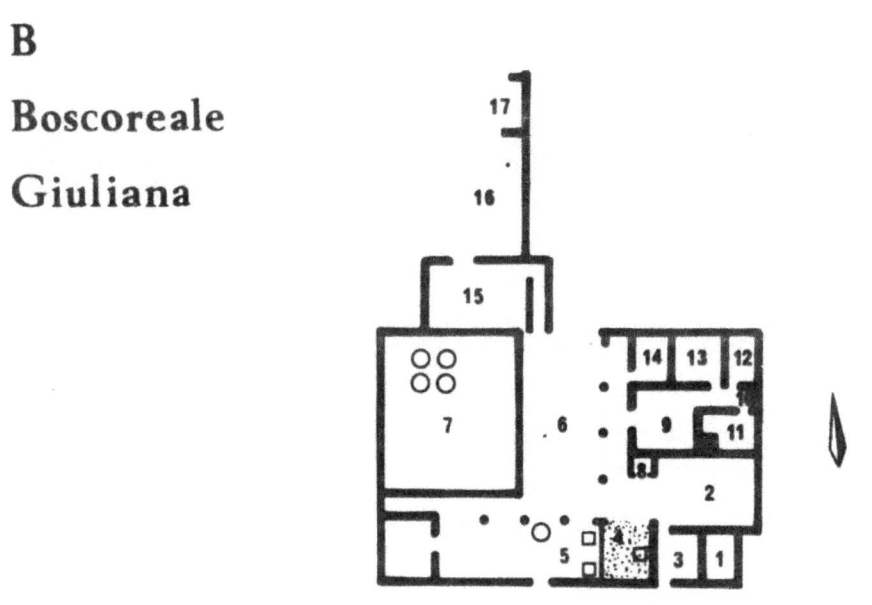

Fig. 5a. Boscoreale Pisanella (after Pasqui). Scale 1:500.

- 1. Courtyard
- 2. Anteroom
- 3-5. Domestic rooms
- 6. Tool-room
- 7. Kitchen
- 8. ? Stable
- 9-12. Bath rooms
- 13. Press-room
- 14/15. Pressing platforms
- 16. Room with hand mill
- 17. Milling room
- 18. Press-room
- 19. Barn
- 20. Threshing floor
- 21. Dolia store

Fig. 5b. Boscoreale Giuliana (after Sogliano). Scale 1:500.

- 1. Lararium
- 2/3. Domestic rooms
- 4. Pressing platform
- 5. Press-room
- 6. Courtyard
- 7. Dolia store
- 8. Store-room
- 9. Kitchen
- 10. Latrine
- 11-13. Uncertain use
- 14. Cubiculum
- 15. Uncertain use (? barn)
- 16 Threshing floor
- 17. Barn

numerous dolia, set into the ground, which served as fermentation vats for wine, or storage jars for oil. Close to the storage rooms are the pressrooms (Fig. 5a, 13; Fig. 5b, 5), containing lever presses and more dolia used as receptacles for the grape-juice or oil. The absence in these rooms of decantation vats and mills, found at numerous other farms and associated with the processing of olive oil (see below, Chapter V) seems to indicate that at these Boscoreale farms the main product was wine and not oil. The Villa Pisanella, however, must have processed some oil to judge from the presence of a second smaller press-room and adjoining milling-room (Fig. 5a, 17 and 18); the oil was probably allowed to settle in the collecting vessel beside the press and then transferred to the dolia store.

That both these farms produced grain is evident from the presence at each of a threshing floor (Fig. 5a, 20; Fig. 5b, 16) and barn. In the one case (Fig. 5b, 17), the identification of the barn seems certain. It is placed at a distance from the main farm building as a precaution against fire, and is conveniently placed next to the threshing floor (Varro, R.R. I.13.5).[6] The room immediately adjoining the threshing floor of the Villa Pisanella (Fig. 5a, 19) may also have been a barn (nubilarium). It contained fragments of bean-straw and parts of a wagon.[7] Over this room, and extending over the east corner of the building, was an upper storey, which may have been used as sleeping accommodation for some of the farm's personnel, or as storage space for dry products. An upper storey also existed over part of the portico, to the southwest of the courtyard and here, in view of its proximity to the residential rooms of the ground floor, were probably the owner's sleeping rooms. There is no reason to suppose that the upper storey here housed a room for a vilicus.[8] In fact, the association of this farm, where the management was probably in the hands of the owner and his family, with the Catonian type of slave-run farm under the control of a slave manager — such as Brehaut makes[9] — is surely incorrect. It will be seen later (below, Chapter IV) that the capitalist enterprise, with its slave-gangs and slave manager, required a different sort of architecture.

Another farmhouse which, although only partially excavated, appears to have had a character similar to these Boscoreale farms is one near Civitavecchia in Etruria (Cat. 17). Identifiable in the north-west corner of the building are a large kitchen and an adjacent bath suite. The latter forms part of a major reconstruction of the farmhouse around the middle of the 1st century B.C. The location of the bath next to the kitchen is similar to the arrangement in the Villa Pisanella at Boscoreale.[10] The farm may have had an internal court and portico, judging from the scattered remnants of what appear to be stone pier- or column-bases. The north-east wing of the building perhaps contained the working farm. As has been noted above, a large barn stood apart from the farmhouse, and this may indicate that cereal crops were an important product. The archaeological evidence, however, is insufficient to assess the agricultural functions of the farm.

What are the architectural traditions behind the design of this type of farm, and how does this rural architecture of the late Republic correspond to the domestic architecture of the same period? Firstly, there appears to be in the design of the Boscoreale farms, as in the case of some of the small farmsteads discussed in the last chapter, an echo of certain features encountered in the domestic architecture of the Greek world. The arrangement of court, portico and residence reflects an arrangement seen in many of the houses at Olynthus. The portico of the Roman farms fulfils a function similar to that of the Greek παστάς, lying between the range of domestic rooms and the court. Like the παστάς, the portico generally lies on the northerly side of the court, as in the Villa Pisanella (Fig. 5a) and in other partially excavated farmhouses in the region south of Vesuvius, such as those in the contrada Spinelli (Cat. 31) and contrada Minutella (Cat. 37). Where the portico extends around a second or third side of the court, the northern part of it retains a position of predominance, as in the case of the Greek παστάς/peristyle houses. A second feature of the farms is their large kitchens, which occupy a position of importance in the living quarters. This is evident not only in the two Boscoreale farms, but also in other farmhouses in the vicinity, such as the one in contrada Spinelli, mentioned above, and in another in contrada Crapolla (Cat. 30). These kitchens, as has been noted above, may represent the survival of an older rural architecture, comprising a hall with central hearth and open roof, an arrangement which had by now been adapted and assimilated into the vocabulary of domestic town architecture in the form of the town-house atrium.

Discussing the plans of the Boscoreale farms, R. C. Carrington suggests that "this type of farmhouse shows no trace of having been influenced by the plan of the town house".[11] By this, one may suppose that he means that these farms lack the principal features and characteristics of contemporary urban dwellings, such as their axial arrangement, the developed atrium and tablinum. Certainly, these features are conspicuously absent in the Boscoreale farms. There are, however, other farmhouses, some of them contemporary, in which these features of the town house do appear. One of these is the farmhouse at Camerelle in Calabria (Cat. 9. Fig. 6). The house was built around a central peristyle, and preserves in its plan some degree of axial symmetry. To the west of the peristyle was a room (Fig. 6, 11) which may have been an atrium. Its central feature was described by the excavator as an impluvium, though she suggests that this area was possibly an open court.[12] The function of each of the other rooms of the farmhouse was not established with certainty, though it does appear that the rooms to the north of the peristyle were for the most part used for agricultural purposes. A press-room in this part of the farm (Fig. 6, 7) probably contained two presses, while in another room (Fig. 6, 2) a second press and fragments of dolia were discovered.[13]

There are several other farmhouses which include an atrium and impluvium in the idiom of town house architecture. These include a farm at Vittimose, near Buccino (Cat. 41), one at Gragnano (Cat. 13) and one excavated near the Via Tiberina in the vicinity of Rome (Cat. 38). The dates of these atrium/impluvium farmhouses show an interesting range; the Camerelle farm dates from the 1st century B.C. while the atrium of the Via Tiberina farm may be pre-Augustan. The Gragnano and Vittimose farms would seem both to belong to the 1st century A.D. Another atrium farmhouse, however, excavated at Salapia in Apulia (Cat. 29) can be dated at least to the early second century B.C. Carrington's claim that "in the first century A.D., as the influence of the town house grew stronger, the atrium too found its way into the country" needs to be revised;[14] the atrium in fact appears in farmhouses of an earlier period, and was evidently a feature of farmhouse architecture of the Republican as well as the Imperial period.

FIG 6

Camerelle

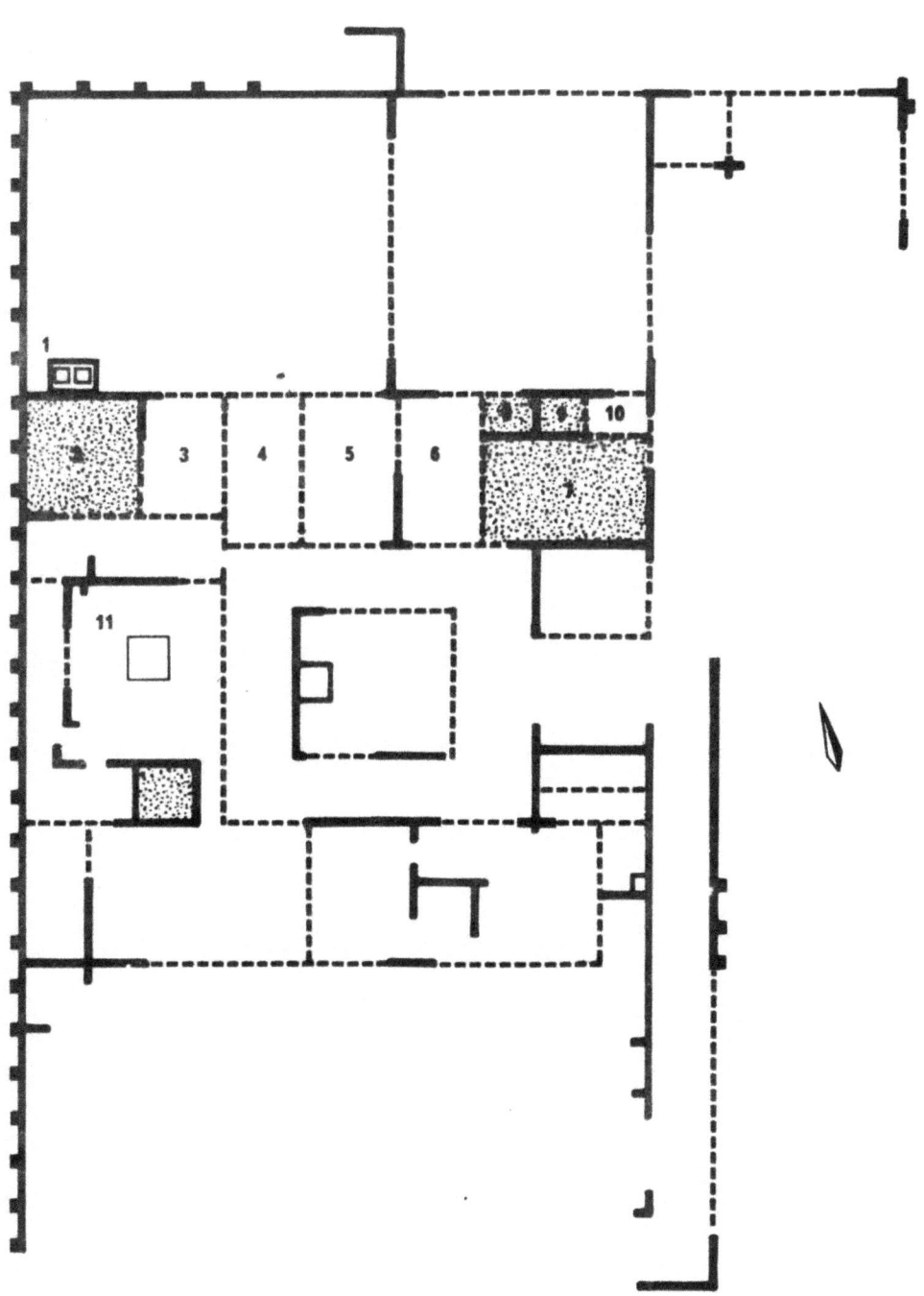

Fig. 6.　　Camarelle (after Bertocchi).　Scale 1:500.

    1.　　　Settling tanks
    2.　　　Press-room
    3-6.　　Uncertain use
    7.　　　Press-room
    8-10.　 Settling tanks
    11.　　 ? Atrium

Fig. 7a.　Portaccia (after Romanelli).　Scale 1:500.

    1.　　Store-room
    2.　　Settling tank
    3.　　? Press-room
    4.　　Kitchen

Fig. 7b.　Villa of Publius Fannius Sinistor (after Barnabei).
Scale 1:500.

    1.　　　　? Unloading bay
    2.　　　　Press-room
    3.　　　　Lararium
    4.　　　　? Barn
    5/6.　　　Kitchen
    7.　　　　Latrine
    8-10.　　 Bath-rooms
    11/12/14.　Domestic rooms
    13.　　　　Tablinum

FIG 7

A Portaccia

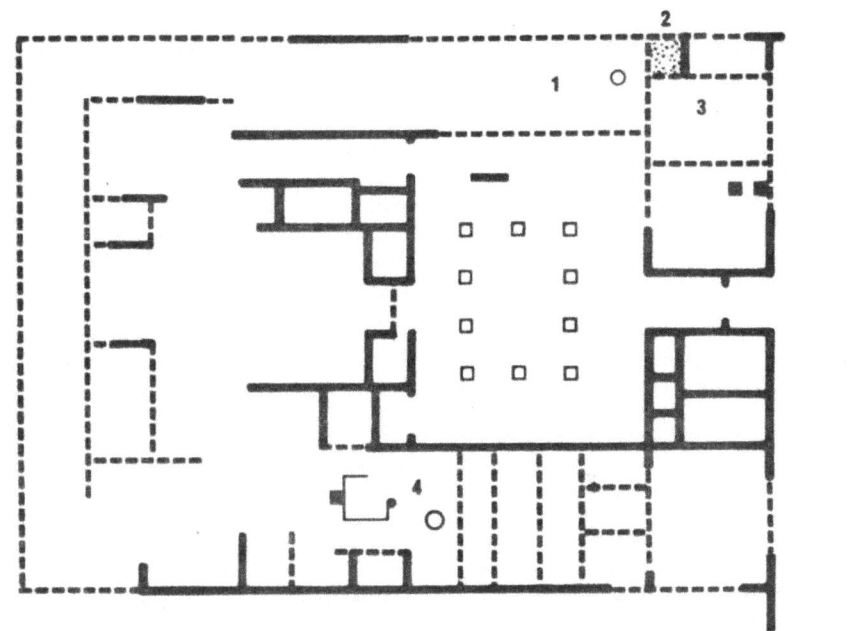

B Villa of Publius Fannius Sinistor

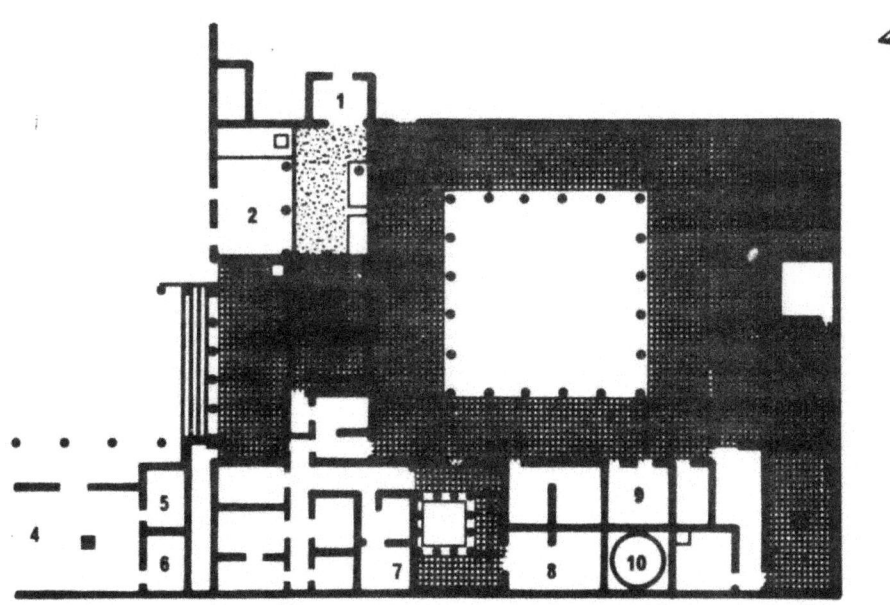

An architectural concept similar to that at Camarelle can be seen in a poorly recorded farmhouse at Portaccia near Tarquinia (Cat. 21. Fig. 7a). Here again the building is characterised by its axial plan, with a centrally placed peristyle and entrance. Though a detailed report of the excavation is lacking it appears that a kitchen (Fig. 7a, 4) and perhaps other domestic rooms were located to the south of the peristyle, while the rooms to the north were used for agricultural purposes. These included a long room (Fig. 7a, 1) which contained fragments of dolia and seems to have served as a barn or large storeroom. To the east of this were found the remains of what appears to be an oil settling tank (Fig. 7a, 2) and it would therefore seem probable that the room adjacent to the tank (room 3) housed the farm's pressing machinery.

Such axially planned peristyle farmhouses as those at Camarelle and Portaccia, and the farms like those at Vittimose and Salapia which include in their design an atrium, display some of the characteristics of contemporary town house architecture. In this respect they contrast with the Boscoreale farmhouses which we have examined. Indeed there seem to be two distinct architectural genres, two kinds of rural architecture, of which Vitruvius, writing at the end of the first century B.C., was clearly aware. Having outlined the requirements of the villa rustica, he advises (D.A. VI.6.5) that a farmhouse designed to include some of the architectural elegance of a town house be built according to the symmetrical canons of the latter:

> si quid delicatius in villis faciendum fuerit, ex symmetriis quae in urbanis supra scripta sunt constituta, ita struantur, uti sine impeditione rusticae utilitatis aedificentur.

For Vitruvius then a farmhouse may be built with some of the characteristics of town house architecture, but clearly this is an option. At least as early as the mid 1st century B.C., and probably earlier, this option was being adopted in some farm architecture.

NOTES

1. For a full bibliography of this, the best known of the Campanian "villae rusticae", see Appendix A.

2. J. Day, 'Agriculture in the life of Pompeii', Yale Classical Studies III (1932), p. 180 ff. His estimate of c. 100 iugera is very suspect. It presupposes that all the dolia were filled to capacity each year, which may not have been the case. The estimate also excludes the possibility of further (unexcavated) storage facilities. Day's calculations are rejected by Frank, E.S.A.R. V, p. 172, p. 264f., who lowers the size of the estate to 10 - 15 iugera, and by R. Duncan-Jones, The economy of the Roman Empire, Cambridge 1974, p. 45, note 3; cf. P. Castren, Ordo Populusque Pompeianus, Rome 1975, p. 53.

3. Crova, Edilizia, p. 77.

4. See chapter 1, note 28.

5. H. F. De Cou, Antiquities from Boscoreale in the Field Museum of Natural History, Chicago 1912.

6. Vitruvius, D.A., VI. VI. 5 ('Horrea, fenilia, pistrina extra villam facienda videntur, ut ab ignis periculo sint villae tutiores — graneries, hay-lofts and bakeries should be away from the farmhouse, so that the houses are safer from the danger of fire'); for example the barn of the late Republican farm at Monna Felice (Cat 17), which is at a good distance from the farmhouse.

7. White, R. F., p. 425. The word nubilarium literally means a shed or barn in which to store corn out of the rain. Varro, R. R., I. XIII. 5 ('Id secundum aream faciendum, ubi triturus sis frumentum, magnitudine pro modo fundi, ex una parte apertum, et id ab area, quo et in trituram proruere facile possis et, si nubilare coepit, inde ut rursus celeriter reicere — it (sc. the shed) should be built next to the threshing floor, of a size in proportion to the farm, open on the side facing the threshing floor, so that you can easily throw out the corn for threshing and, if it begins to get cloudy, throw it back in again in a hurry').

8. Thus White, R. F., p. 425.

9. E. Brehaut, Cato the Censor on farming, New York 1933, p. 30.

10. Vitruvius, D. A., VI.6.2. ('Balnearia item coniuncta sint culinae — the bathrooms should be next to the kitchen'). See further, E. Fabbricotti, 'I bagni nelle prime ville romane', Cronache Pompeiane II (1976), pp. 29-111.

11. Carrington, 1934, pp. 261-280; idem, Pompeii, Oxford 1936, p. 90.

12. Bertocchi, op.cit., p. 143.
13. Bertocchi, op.cit., p. 147; see also below Chapter V.
14. Carrington, op.cit. (1936), p. 94.

CHAPTER III

RURAL VILLAS

The kind of farm described by Columella (D.R.R., I.VI) comprises several distinct parts; a residence (villa urbana), a working farm (villa rustica) and storage facilities (villa fructuaria). These three elements were, of course, common to most farmhouses of whatever size, although the means by which the architect chose to incorporate them into his farm design could vary greatly. The compact single-structure farms, where the different facilities were all combined into a single architectural design, have been discussed in the last chapter. We must now consider a group of villas built on a larger scale, wherein the different parts of the villa each constitute a separate structure or group of structures.

The simplest form of separation can be seen at the San Rocco villa (Cat. 27, Fig. 8), where the residence and the working farm form architecturally independent units placed side by side and separated only by a roadway which gives access to the main entrance of the residence and to one of the two farmyards. The whole complex thus forms two distinct parts: the residence, in the form of a series of rooms ranged around a central peristyle, and the farm, with its various facilities flanking two interconnected yards. The presence of porticos on the southwest and northwest sides of the residence, together with the internal peristyle, recalls the ambulationes prescribed by Columella for the villa urbana (D.R.R., I.VI.2). Similarly, the cubicula on these same sides of the building, while not necessarily arranged for seasonal use, as Columella suggests, nevertheless form an impressive range.

The two farmyards appear to have been used for separate agricultural activities.[1] That to the west was probably used for livestock: it is located close to the main north entrance and thus affords easy access to the country; there is a large cistern on its south side and, adjacent to this, a portico which could have been used for stalling animals. The rooms to the north of this yard may have been used to store equipment or as accommodation for personnel. The second yard contained an oil processing plant with, to the north, the pressrooms and to the south the settling tanks. Located between the two yards was a pottery workshop and kiln. Unfortunately, the excavation of the working farm at San Rocco has not yet been published in detail.[2]

Not far removed from the plan of the San Rocco villa is that of a villa excavated at Russi near Ravenna (Cat. 25. Fig. 9). The excavated rooms of the villa urbana occupied the north part of the villa, being ranged mainly to the south and west (and perhaps to the north, though this area was not investigated) of a peristyle. This was flanked to the east by a large barn (for details of which see below, p. 59). Immediately to the south of the villa urbana was a second courtyard around which most of the agricultural facilities of the farm appear

FIG 8

San Rocco Period 3

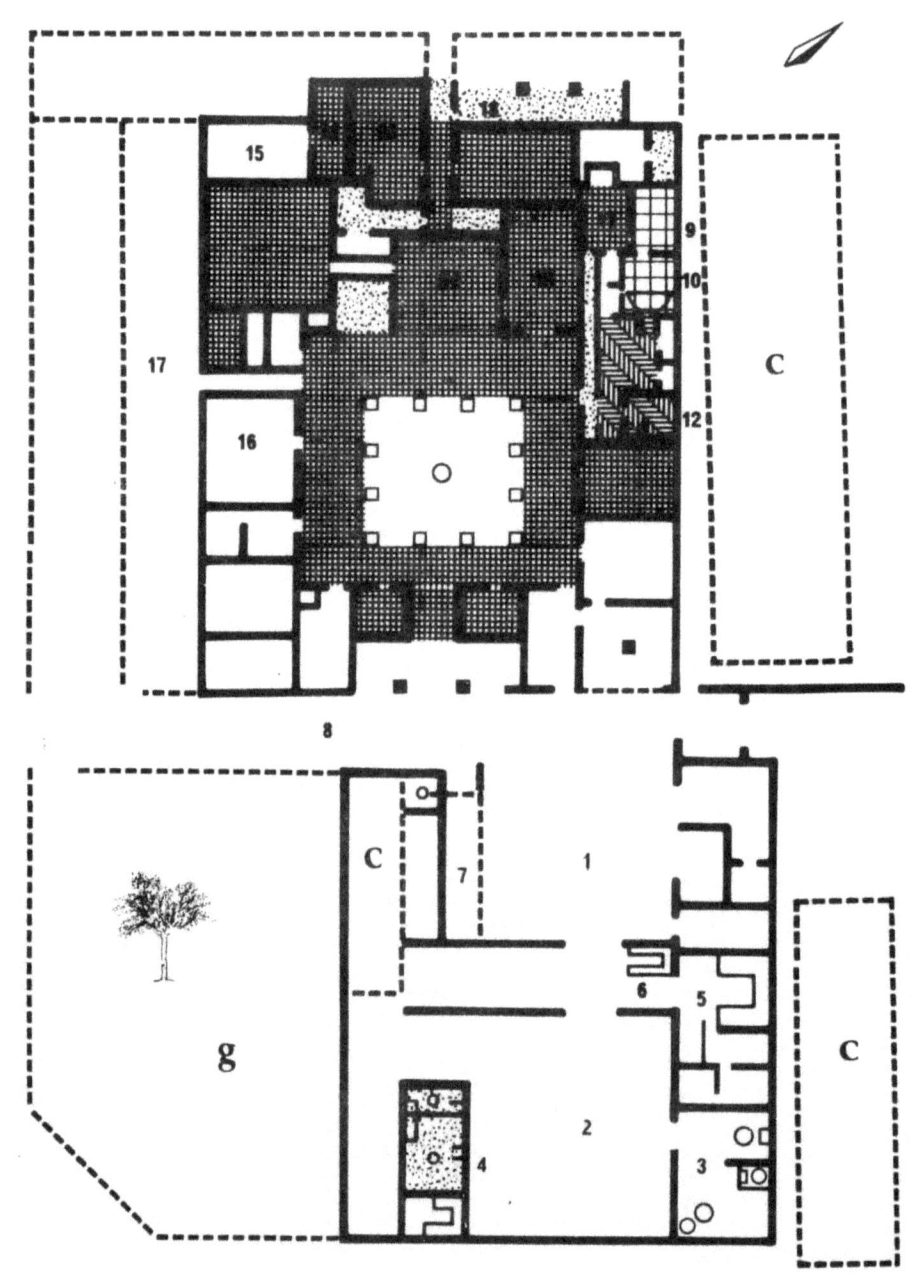

Fig. 8.   San Rocco (after Boethius and Ward-Perkins).   Scale 1:500.

     1/2.   Farmyards
     3.   Press-room
     4.   Settling tanks
     5/6.   Kilns
     7.   Stalls
     8.   Roadway
     9-11.   Bath rooms
     12.   Kitchen
     13-16. Cubicula
     17/18. Porticos
     19.   Triclinium
     20.   Tablinum
     C.   Cisterns
     G.   Garden

Fig. 9.   Russi (after Scagliarini).   Scale 1:500.

     1.   Barn
     2.   ? Grain bins
     3.   Settling tank
     4.   ? Treading floor
     5.   Pond and well-head
     6.   Granary
     7-9.   Porticos

FIG 9

Russi. Period 3

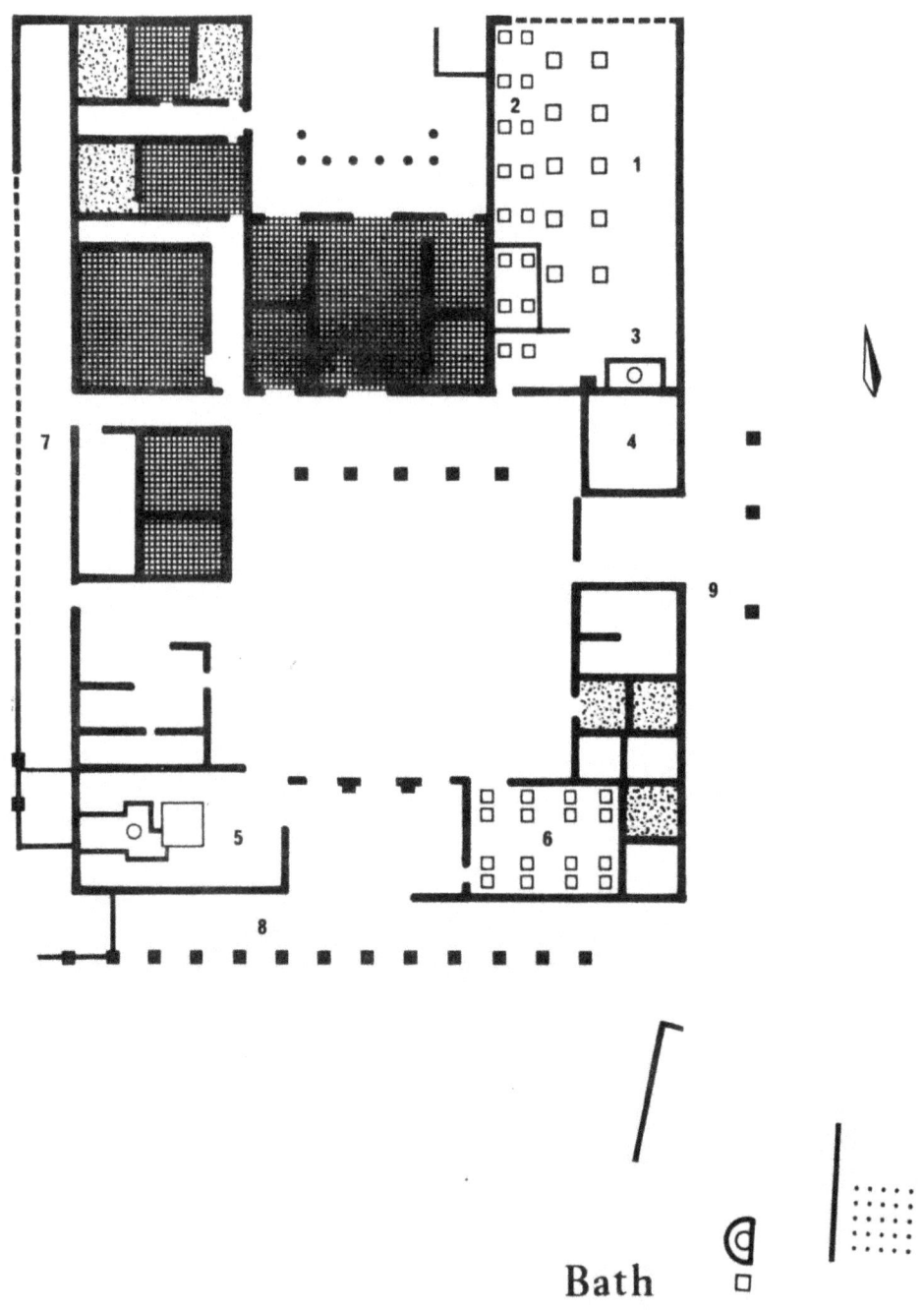

Bath

to have been located. These included a granary (Fig. 9, 6; below, p. 57) and a large room (Fig. 9, 5), perhaps unroofed, containing a central basin which, located just to the east of a well head, may have been a drinking trough for livestock or else perhaps used for soaking lupines for manure or fodder. To the south-east of the villa was located a separate bath building. The separation of the bath house from the villa urbana, partly as a precaution against fire, is a feature which we shall find repeated at a number of large villa sites.[3]

Another similarly designed villa is the so-called "Villa of Publius Fannius Sinistor" excavated towards the end of the nineteenth century at Boscoreale near Pompeii (Cat. 5. Fig. 7b). Although not fully explored, this villa, constructed around the middle of the 1st century B.C., appears to have been planned, like the San Rocco and Russi villas, as an integrated complex with two adjacent and interconnecting courts. To the north the rooms of the villa urbana extended round three sides of a peristyle. These included a centrally placed tablinum (Fig. 7b, 13), more than one triclinium (11 and 12) and a suite of bath rooms (8, 9 and 10). Most of the rooms of the residential part of the villa were sumptuously decorated with mosaics and murals. To the south, at a lower level, was a second colonnaded courtyard which appears to have been flanked by the facilities of the working farm. One of these rooms (Fig. 7b, 2), located between the peristyle of the villa urbana and the courtyard of the villa rustica, was the villa's press-room which contained two presses of the platform type (see below, chapter V). To the west of the press-room was a small room (Fig. 7b, 1) which may have served as an unloading bay for carts bringing olives or grapes to the press-room. Also flanking the courtyard was a large room, only partially excavated (Fig. 7b, 4), which was perhaps a storage barn. This connected with two smaller rooms (5 and 6) which according to Barnabei formed the villa's kitchens.

These three villas all share a similar architectural plan; a villa urbana with a central peristyle forming one of the villa's two main nuclei and a working farm around a second courtyard forming the other. The two are juxtaposed to create an extensive complex which would seem to correspond to the type of elaborate residential farm envisaged by Columella. At other sites a much looser arrangement seems to have been the case. Several villa sites have been identified by scattered structural remains, which suggest a number of independent buildings spread over a wide area. An example of this type of "fragmented" villa is to be seen at Villa Magna near Anagni in the Roman Campagna (Cat. 40. Fig. 10). An inscription of 207 A.D., found at the site, records the construction of a road (deverticulum) which likely served as a driveway for the villa.[4] Of the villa itself some surface remains survive and these suggest the presence of a number of buildings spread over an area of about 0.5 sq km. The structural vestiges to the south of the site (Fig. 10.B) may be the remains of a residential complex (villa urbana). Here a small exedra and related architectural fragments suggest a building of some refinement. The construction of the walls is in opus reticulatum indicating a late Republican or early Imperial date for the building. Nearby was a series of cisterns capable of retaining a large water supply for the villa. At the north of the site more upstanding masonry remains (Fig. 10.A) indicate a second group of buildings. The construction here is in opus reticulatum with bonding courses of brick, suggesting a date in the later 1st or first half of the 2nd century A.D.[5] The function of these buildings is quite uncertain. They may have belonged to a bath complex or were perhaps associated with the agricultural working of the estate.

A comparable villa site is that of "il Casalaccio" recorded in the Ager Veientanus survey (Cat. 7). Here again, the villa was provided with its own paved driveway, nearly 1 km in length, which led from the Via Flaminia. The villa consisted of a number of independently-sited buildings, whose precise function cannot be determined without a more detailed study. The structures which formed the south group of buildings were clearly connected with the water supply of the villa, while the northern building may have been residential—the surface finds from this area included materials for floor mosaics. A third building, located between these two, contained wall mosaics to judge from the surface finds of glass tesserae, but its function can only be guessed.

Another large "fragmented" villa is the early Imperial villa at Cugno dei Vagni (Cat. 10. Fig. 11) in the Siris-Heraclea district of Basilicata. The villa here seems to have extended over a wide area, though the scattered structural remains would require a more thorough examination to determine their relationship. One group of buildings was examined by Lacava in the 19th century and more recent plans of this complex have been published by Quilici and Adamesteanu.[6] This was a bath building situated on the southeast slopes of the hilltop on which the residential part of the villa was sited.

If it be supposed that such villa sites were the centres of fairly extensive estates, one must then ask on what basis their associated land holdings were farmed. In many cases, excavation or surface survey has revealed evidence of elaborate residential building groups, but agricultural facilities have not been detected with any degree of certainty. This may be due to lack of excavation and one could argue that associated farm buildings must have existed in proximity to the villa urbana. The larger the estate, however, the less practicable it would have been to farm the land from a central location. The latifundia of the Imperial age, many of which were probably created by the absorption of smaller holdings and farmsteads, were more probably farmed from a number of scattered farmsteads spread over the extent of the estate, and operated by tenant coloni.[7] We may thus be wrong in expecting always to find agricultural facilities associated with the residential villa which formed the nucleus of the estate. Rather, the farm equipment and storage facilities may have been located in small farmsteads which remained the centres of operation for the farming of the different parts of the estate.

What of the architecture of the big country farms? How does it compare with that of the luxurious maritime and suburban villas, about which we are reasonably well-informed as a result of extensive excavation (much of it in the 18th and 19th centuries) and from representations in Roman mural art?[8] Grimal has summarized the main architectural features of these villas; the porticos, towers, pavilions, baths and recreational facilities. Some, such as the gymnasia and stadia, belong clearly to the world of luxury and entertainment.[9] Others, however, although seen in their most exaggerated form in the pleasure villas of the Campanian littoral, also find expression in the architecture of the larger Roman farms. For example, the ambulationes

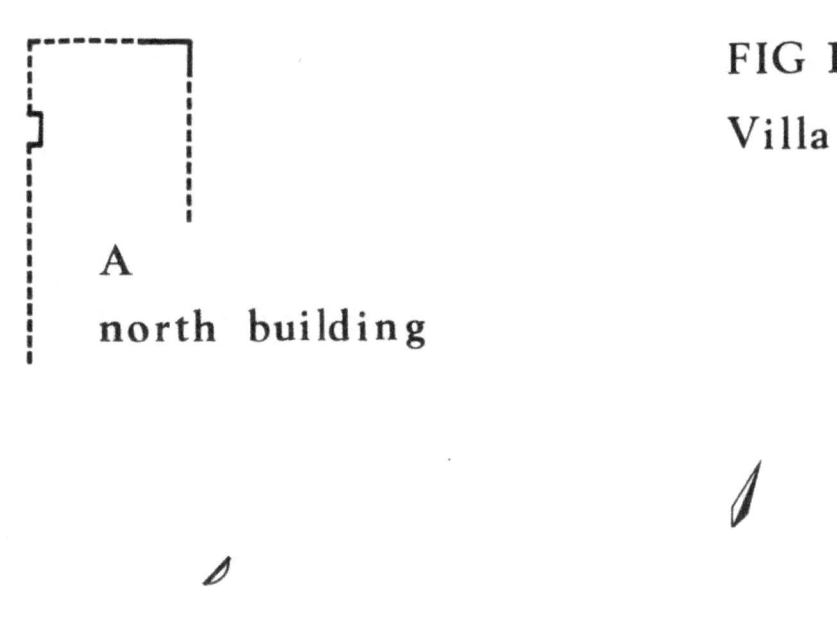
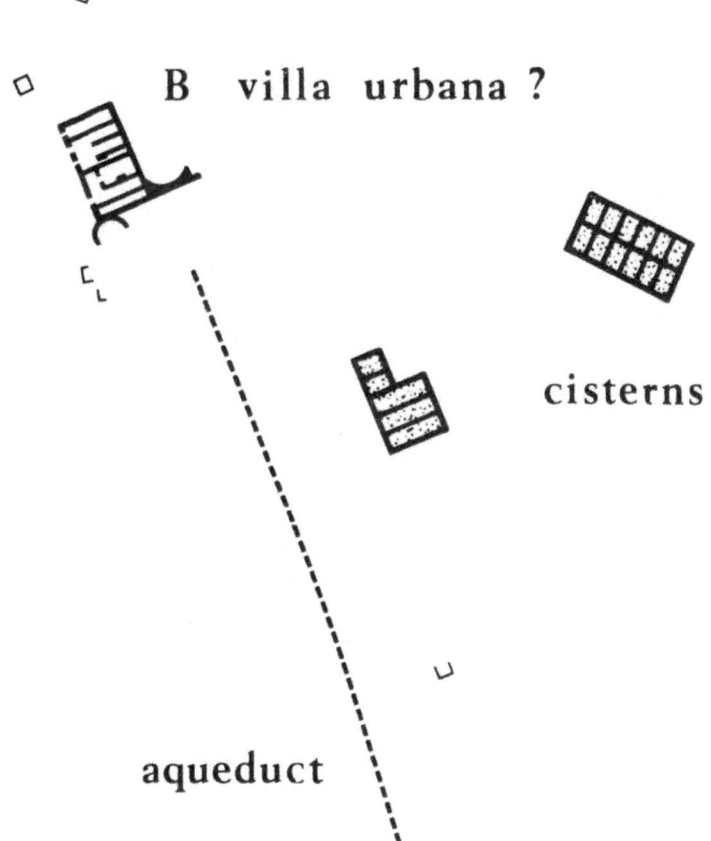

FIG 11
Cugno Dei Vagni

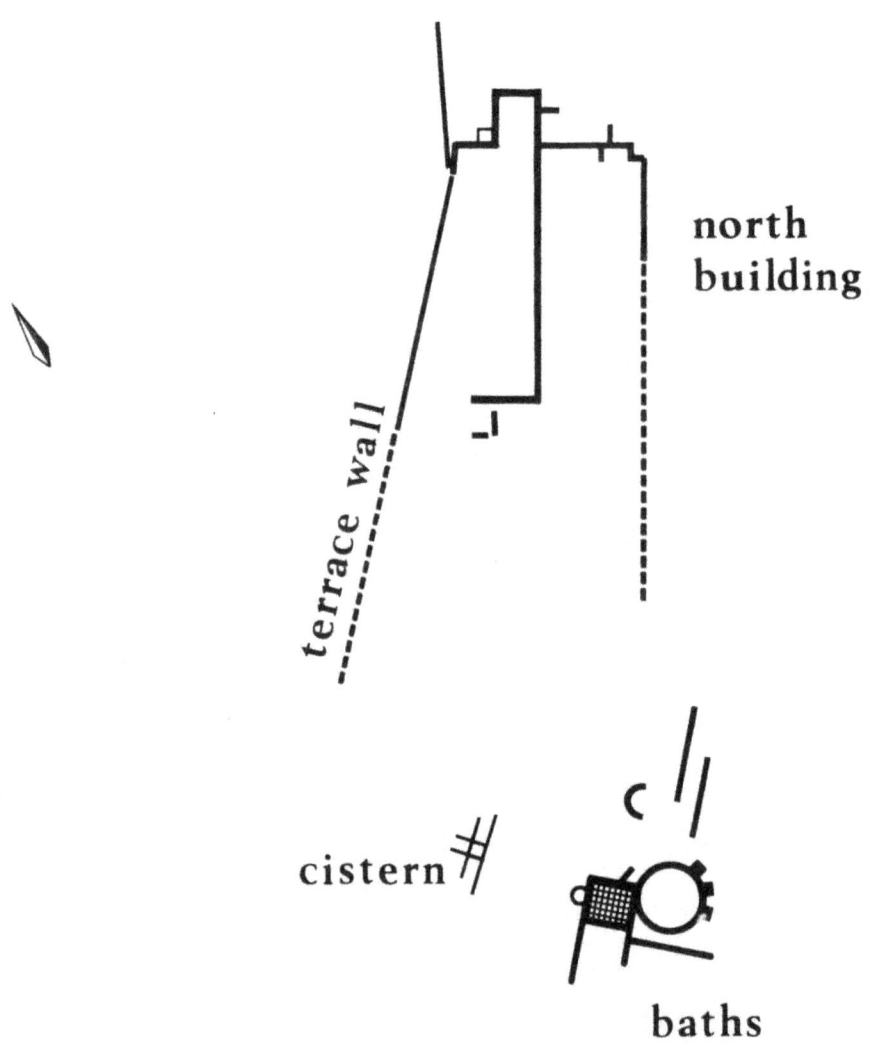

(colonnaded promenades) seen in numerous luxury villas are also found on a reduced scale in some of the rural villas. As mentioned above, Columella advises the inclusion of such in the villa urbana of his model farm (D.R.R., I. VI. 2). The flanking porticos of the San Rocco villa have already been mentioned in this respect; at Russi, too, three sides of the complex were flanked by long corridors or walkways, which appear to have been colonnaded. The rural villa at Salapia (Apulia) (Cat. 29), Hellenistic in origin, which seems to have included agricultural buildings sited independently from the villa urbana, also had a lengthy colonnaded walk extending along the eastern perimeter of the complex. Another feature of the luxury villas were the diaetae, which Grimal associates with the various tower-like pavilions which, as we know from excavation and from wall-paintings, graced the gardens of the most luxurious villas.[10] That towers existed in farm architecture too seems fairly certain. Varro (R.R., III.3.6.) speaks of pigeons in turribus, and the kind of rustic towers depicted amidst the architectural forms in a mural from the Villa of Publius Fannius Sinistor may reflect an actual feature of contemporary farm design (Plate 1b).[11] The towers have sloping tiled roofs, with pigeon cotes located beneath the eaves, above what seem to be storage lofts.

More certainly identified are the independent bath blocks which have been found in the vicinity of some of the larger farms, such as those at Russi and at Cugno dei Vagni. The separation of the bath from the main body of the villa was a planning feature which became increasingly common with the luxury villas, according to Grimal.[12] The isolation of the baths resulted both from their greater architectural elaboration and increased social importance, and from the fact that the heating systems presented something of a fire hazard and were therefore well located away from the main body of the villa.

The large villa complexes discussed here illustrate how wealthy landowners in the Imperial period sought to bring a degree of luxury and fashionable elegance to their country estates, a tendency which had been condemned by Varro (R.R., II.13.6) in the early Augustan period, but which was regarded by Columella as acceptable and necessary for the status-minded landowner. The farm envisaged by Columella is more than just an agricultural centre. It is also a country residence of some elegance, where an architectural style which had become established in the suburban and maritime villas of Italy was introduced into the rural estates of the rich.

NOTES

1. Varro, R.R., I. XIII. 3, suggests two courtyards for a large farm, one with a central drinking pond for livestock, the other with a cistern for soaking lupines (used for cattle fodder).

2. With the exception of the oil separation tanks, of which a plan has been published in the interim reports; P.B.S.R. XX (1965) pp. 62-5; N. Sc. 1965, p. 246.

3. See below p. 37.

4. C.I.L. X. No. 5909.

5. Compare, for example, similar concrete facing at the Imperial villa at Castel Gandolfo (Albanum); M. E. Blake, Roman Construction in Italy, Vol. II (1959), pp. 134-5, 161; Vol. III (1973), pp. 257-8.

6. M. Lacava, Topografia e storia di Metaponto, Napoli 1891, pp. 17-20; Adamesteanu, Basilicata Antica, Rome 1975, p. 224; L. Quilici, Siris - Heraclea: Forma Italiae Reg. III. Vol. I., Rome 1967, pp. 136-8.

7. cf. Horace, Epistles I. XIV. 2, where he praises his 'quinque boni patres'. The excavation of a large rural villa near Licenza, reputedly belonging to the author, revealed no traces of an agricultural quarter or of farm equipment; G. Lugli, 'La villa Sabina di Orazio', M.A. XXXI (1926-7), pp. 457-599; idem, La villa d'Orazio nella valle del Licenza, Rome 1930.

8. For good summaries of the luxury villas see: P. Grimal, Les Jardins Romains (2nd. ed.), Paris 1969; J. D'Arms, Romans on the Bay of Naples, Cambridge, Mass. 1970. On the graphic evidence: M. Rostovtzeff, 'Die hellenistich-römische architekturlandschaff', Röm. Mitt. XXVI (1911), p. 1ff.; idem, 'Pompeianische landschaften und römische Villen', Jahr. Deut. Arch. Inst. XIX (1904), pp. 10-126.

9. Grimal, op.cit., chapters 7-8.

10. Grimal, op.cit., pp. 259-262; cf. P. Lehmann, Roman wall paintings from Boscoreale, Cambridge, Mass. 1953, pp. 106-8; Ward-Perkins, E.R.A., p. 583, interprets the word as simply meaning a living-room; cf. A.W. Van Buren, 'Laurentinum Plinii Minoris', R.P.A.A. XX (1943-4), pp. 165-192, on Pliny's meaning of 'turres'.

11. Lehmann, op.cit., Plates XIV - XV, p. 99f.

12. Grimal, loc.cit., p. 258 - 'puis, peu à peu, les bains finissent par se détacher de la maison et par former des ensembles complets et bien définis'.

A. Wall painting from the House of the Small Fountain at Pompeii. Later 1st century B.C. or first half of the 1st century A.D.

B. Wall painting from the Villa of Publius Fannius Sinistor at Boscoreale. Second half of the 1st century B.C.

CHAPTER IV

SLAVERY AND FARMS

The employment of slaves as a source of labour on farms is a fundamental principle in the works of the Roman agronomists. The system of intensive plantation agriculture outlined by Cato depended on a slave workforce and a slave overseer, and the slave-run farm remained the basis for the works of Cato's successors. Columella, writing in the 1st century A.D., presents his readers with a comprehensive analysis of this type of slave-operated estate.[1]

The sources imply two categories of rural slaves, servi soluti and servi vincti.[2] Whether the latter's condition was permanent or not is uncertain. Cato mentions chained slaves only once, in the context of rations (D.A. 56). Columella indicates that shackling was a punitive measure (D.R.R. 1.8.17), but this does not mean that it was not a permanent condition for some. The construction of an underground dungeon (ergastulum), which Columella recommends (D.R.R. 1.6.3), would require considerable expense, which could hardly be justified for occasional confinement.[3] However, it may be supposed that the structural requirements of a farm housing large numbers of slaves, of whichever kind, will have been different from those of the family farm operated by a resident owner with a few family slaves and hired labour.[4] The need to accommodate the slave force would doubtless have an important effect on the design of the farm buildings. Cato and Varro both mention the slaves' cellae (D.A. 14; R.R. 1.13), referring to the small rooms in which servi soluti were housed. The living conditions of the slaves were doubtless rudimentary, considering the attitudes of some of the sources: 'The slaves differ only from the working animals in the fact that the former are gifted with speech, while the latter are inarticulate.'[5] Although a few farm buildings do provide some evidence for the ways in which a slave force might be accommodated, study of these remains has been quite inadequate, and Robert Etienne is right in stressing the need for 'une analyse archéologique des villas d'Italie et du monde Romain pour mieux cerner le problème de l'extension du mode de production esclavagiste'.[6]

Slave accommodation is perhaps best seen in the so-called 'Villa of L. Claudius Eutychus' excavated at Boscoreale in 1903-5 (Cat. 6. Fig. 12a). The excavated portion of this building appears as two distinct parts: firstly there was a residential quarter, a lavishly decorated villa urbana, which, it has been suggested, at one time belonged to Agrippa Postumus. Immediately adjacent to this, on a slightly lower level, was a compound which contained the slaves' quarters. There was no evidence here of any agricultural facilities, and it is possible that the compound housed a force of domestic rather than agricultural slaves. With only a partial excavation of the building it is impossible to distinguish. The main entrance to the compound was flanked to the

FIG 12

A
Villa of Tiberius Claudius Eutychus

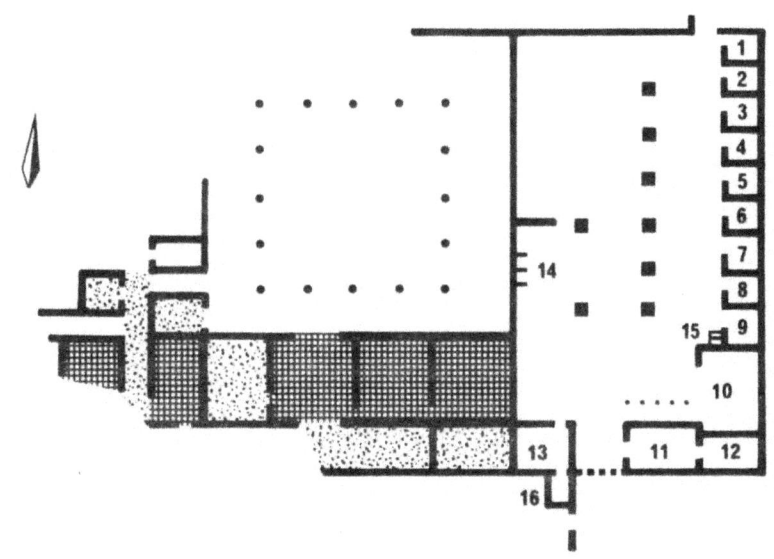

B
Gragnano

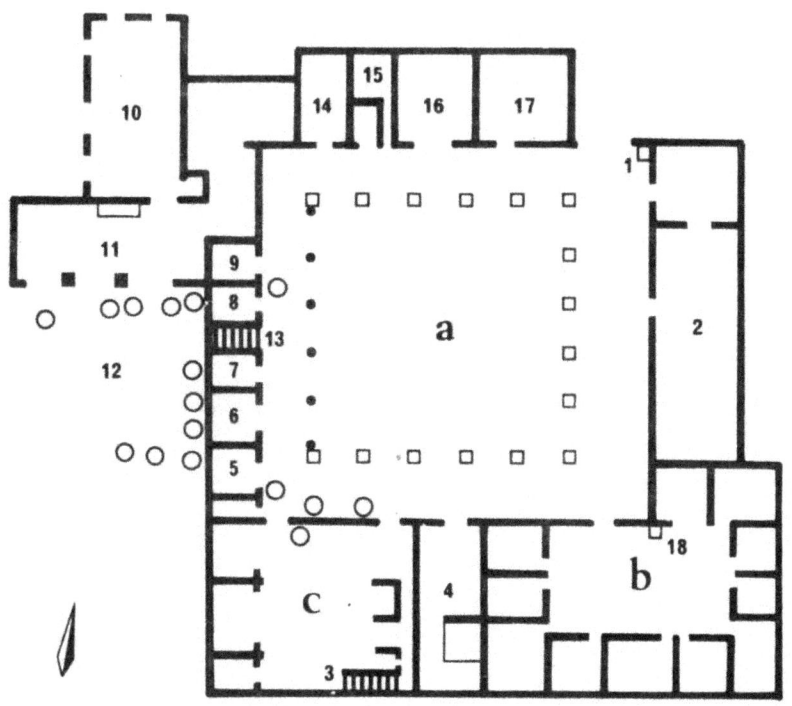

Fig. 12a. Villa of Tiberius Claudius Eutychus (after Della Corte).
Scale 1:500.

    1-9.   Staves' cellae
    10.   Stable
    11-12.   ? Overseer's rooms
    13.   ? Master's office
    14.   Ovens
    15.   Stairs
    16.   Latrine

Fig. 12b. Gragnano (after Della Corte). Scale 1:500.

    1.   Drinking trough
    2.   Cattle-shed/Stable
    3.   Stairs
    4.   Bakery
    5-9.   Slaves' cellae
    10.   Press-room
    11.   Store-shed
    12.   Dolia store
    13.   Stairs
    14-17.   Uncertain use
    18.   Oven

Fig. 13a. Boscoreale Giuliana (after Della Corte). Scale 1:500.

    1-4.   ? Slaves' cellae
    5.   Latrine
    6.   ? Kitchen
    7.   Milling room
    8-11.   Uncertain use
    12.   Store-room
    13.   Barn

Fig. 13b. Vicovaro (after Gatti). Scale 1:500.

    1.   Store-room
    2.   Granary
    3/4.   Press-rooms.
    5.   Settling tank
    6-8.   ? Slave accommodation
    9-12.   Uncertain use

east by a small room (Fig. 12a, 11) from which movements through the gateway could easily be observed. This may well have been occupied by the overseer, thus according with Varro's advice: 'vilici proxime ianuam cellam esse oportet, eumque scire, qui introet aut exeat noctu quidve ferat' (R.R. 1.13). The discovery here of a set of iron stocks may imply that the room was used to confine slaves, though it was not an ergastulum in the Columellan sense of the word. The room on the other side of the gateway (Fig. 12a, 13) is more problematic; unlike any other room around the compound, its walls were decorated with figured paintings, which would seem to relate it more to the residential part of the villa than to the slaves' quarters. The room gave access to a latrine and to the chambers beneath the terrace of the residential rooms. It was most probably an office used by the master of the house.[7]

The most interesting feature of the compound is the row of nine small (2.8 x 1.9 m) and uniform rooms which occupy the east side. These, it would seem, were the slaves' cellae. Each is identical in plan and simplicity. The floors were of trodden earth, the walls faced with plain monochrome plaster. Each room had a single window, and a small niche in the wall for a lamp. There was also a small hearth near the entrance to each room. Above this row of cellae was a second storey reached by a stairway, the base of which was found during excavation (Fig. 12a, 15).[8]

A parallel sort of arrangement can be seen in another of the Campanian farms, found at Gragnano (Cat. 12. Fig. 12b). Rostovtzeff called this farm 'an agricultural factory run by slaves'.[9] To the west of the main courtyard (Fig. 12b, a) was a row of small uniform rooms (Fig. 12b, 5-9) which could well have been slave accommodation. They correspond in size fairly closely with those of the Boscotrecase farm (the cellae all measure approximately 3 x 2 m). An upper storey is again evident. Some of the rooms surrounding the small court (Fig. 12b, b) may also have housed part of the slave force. The discovery of a set of stocks in the second small court (Fig. 12b, c) suggests that facilities existed for shackling slaves, though again not an ergastulum in the Columellan sense, since there was no room flanking the court which remotely corresponds to Columella's slave dungeon. At the south side of courtyard C a stairway led to an upper storey, possibly used for the storage of grain for use in the bakery below (Fig. 12b, 4).[10] Here no doubt part of the slave force was employed.[11] Others were engaged in the various other agricultural activities of the farm, which included viticulture and dairy.

Crova has suggested that the Gragnano farm represents only a part of a larger complex, which would have included the owner's residence (the villa urbana).[12] However in default of evidence to support this it may also be hypothesised that the excavated building at Gragnano, in every respect a utilitarian building, was the working centre of a fairly large estate ('not more than 250 iugera in extent');[13] that operation of the estate was entrusted to a resident vilicus (overseer) with a labour force of slaves who were housed within the farm in a number of purposely constructed cellae; that the estate was run as a capitalist enterprise and owned by an absentee landlord, who made periodic tours of inspection (Cato D.A. 11.1).[14]

Two smaller farm buildings deserve mention here in as much as their excavated remains suggest that they too were operated in their owner's

FIG 13

A

Boscoreale Giuliana

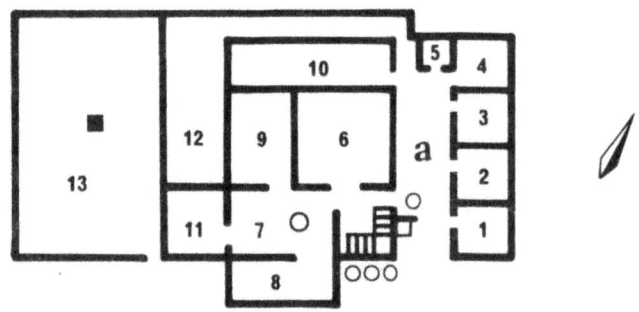

B

Vicovaro

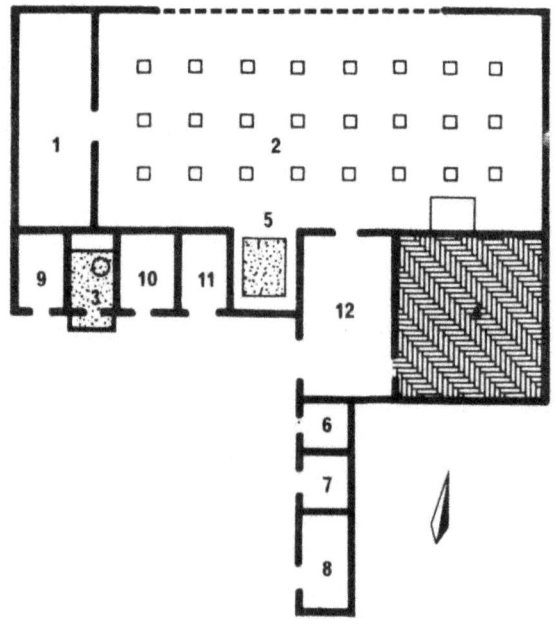

absence by a small workforce of slaves. One is a building excavated at Prato La Corte, near Vicovaro in Lazio, and published by Lugli in 1926 (Cat. 39. Fig. 13b).[15] The largest feature of the building is a spacious granary (Fig. 13b, 2) - discussed below in Chapter VI - recalling Cato's emphasis on the need for good storage facilities, so that produce may be kept to await a good market price (D.A. III.2). To the south of this are ranged a series of smaller rooms, some of which show clear evidence for their use: press-rooms (3 and 4) and an oil settling vat (5).[16] The south wing of the building contained three rooms (Fig. 13b, 6, 7 and 8) which, according to the excavator, formed the living quarters of the farm.[17] Indeed they could have provided a simple form of accommodation for the personnel of the farm. The measurements of the two smaller rooms (6 and 7), 3.3 x 2.6 m, compare well with those of the slave cellae of the farms at Boscotrecase and Gragnano discussed above. Details of construction are not provided in Lugli's account, though it seems that the rooms lacked paved floors and that the walls were unplastered.

Similar conditions appear to have existed at a farm excavated at Boscoreale in 1904 (Cat. 2. Fig. 13a). The plan is of the 1st century A.D. building, and shows how an earlier building was enlarged to provide considerably more storage space. The three largest rooms (Fig. 13a, 10, 12 and 13) were used to store produce and equipment: 10 may have been a wine store, while in 13 a stock of chestnut stakes was found, which were being stored for use as vine-props.[18] The line of small rooms, measuring 3.0 x 3.5 m, along the north-east side of the building provided living quarters for the farm's personnel. These rooms were apparently crudely finished ('rustica e disadorna') and their uniform simplicity suggests that they could have been cellae for a resident slave force.

Neither of these smaller farms is furnished with the kind of 'slave dormitories' which are to be seen in the Boscotrecase and Gragnano farms. However, the series of small, uniform and undecorated rooms which they both contain, though not great in number, may have been slaves' cellae. At each farm the owner of the land appears to have invested his capital mainly in the agricultural equipment of the farm, providing only rudimentary accommodation for the farm's personnel; this would suggest that the farms were designed to be operated in their owner's absence by a small slave force under supervision.

Reference may also be made here to the recent excavations of the rural 'Villa of the Volusii Saturnini' at Lucus Feroniae, north-east of Rome.[19] Although the full extent of this building has not yet been established, excavation has uncovered the remains of a large residential building which is an Augustan reconstruction and enlargement of an earlier Republican villa. The rebuilding included the addition of a sizeable colonnaded courtyard, flanked on at least two sides by ranges of small uniform chambers. These rooms, it has been suggested, were designed to house the villa's resident workforce of slaves.[20] More rooms of a similar size flank a second pillared courtyard, adjacent to and connecting with the large yard, and these too may have provided further accommodation for the villa's personnel. This second courtyard was paved, probably to facilitate the movement of carts and animals. For details of any farming equipment and facilities found at the site, however, and an interpretation of the agricultural economy of the villa, we must await a full report of the excavations.

The prevalence of the slave-run farm in Italy cannot be determined from the small amount of archaeological evidence discussed above. Rostovtzeff used the Gragnano and Boscoreale farms as sufficient evidence to create his category of 'factory farms', a classification adopted by Carrington and others. Certainly there is enough literary evidence to suggest that slave-run farms with absentee landlords were a part of the Italian landscape, but until excavation has provided more evidence for slave accommodation on farms our information concerning the ways in which this type of farm was arranged and constructed will remain very limited. The Gragnano farm provides perhaps the best clue. For here there is evidence both of the slave cellae and of the agricultural facilities in which the slave force was employed. However this farm is unique; others like it may have existed in Campania and elsewhere, but until this can be shown by excavation the major source of evidence for the employment of slaves on farms must remain in the literary texts.

NOTES

1. On capitalist systems of farming in Roman Italy see: White, R.F. p. 389f., pp. 401-5; idem, A Bibliography of Roman Farming, Reading 1970, pp. xii-xiv; idem, 'Roman agricultural writers I', Aufstieg und Niedergang der Römischen Welt I:4, Berlin 1973, pp. 439-497; idem, F.E.R.W., p. 213ff.; A. Toynbee, Hannibal's Legacy (2 vols), Oxford 1965, p. 291ff.; M. W. Frederiksen, 'The contribution of archaeology to the agrarian problem of the Gracchan period', Dialoghi di Archeologia (1970-1), Rome 1972, p. 334ff.

2. On chained slaves see: R. Duncan-Jones, The economy of the Roman Empire, Cambridge 1974, pp. 323-4; White, R.F., pp. 361-2; R. Martin, 'Familia rustica: les esclaves chez les agronomes latins', Actes du colloque 1972 sur l'esclavage (Université de Besançon), Paris 1974, pp. 267-297.

3. Columella is the only agricultural author to refer specifically to an ergastulum, which he describes as follows (D.R.R. 1.6.3):

    'quam saluberrimum subterraneum ergastulum, sitque id angustis in lustratum fenestris atque a terra sic editis ne manu contingi possint—an underground dungeon, as wholesome as possible, lit by narrow windows far enough off the ground that they cannot be reached by hand'.

    Nothing corresponding to this has been found by excavation. Elsewhere (D.R.R. I.3.12) he uses the word to refer to the actual slave gangs; cf. Apuleius, Apologia, 47 ('Quindecim liberi homines populus est, totidem servi familia, totidem vincti ergastulum—fifteen free men make a crowd, fifteen slaves make a disciplined crowd, fifteen chained slaves a work force'). For a discussion of the different uses of the word see R. Etienne, 'Recherche sur l'ergastule', Actes du colloque 1972 sur l'esclavage, Paris 1974, pp. 249-266.

4. J. E. Skydsgaard, Den Romerske Villa Rustica, Copenhagen 1961, p. 95f., sees this as the main distinction between Roman farm types; on the one hand the family-run farm, on the other the slave-run farm with an absentee landlord.

5. White, op.cit. (1973), p. 453; Varro, R.R., I.17.

6. Etienne, op.cit., p. 266.

7. A similar well-decorated room which 'intrudes into the service quarter' was found in the Casa dei Dioscuri in Pompeii; L. Richardson Jr., The Casa dei Dioscuri and its painters, M.A.A.R. XXIII 1955. Richardson suggests that the room here was used by the mistress of the house as a place where she 'could work and supervise her slaves at the same time'.

8. The main obstacle to the interpretation of these rooms as cellae for slaves is the nature of the excavated contents of some of the rooms. These included pieces of gold and silver, and even some gems and cameos (Della Corte, N.Sc. 1922, p. 463). Such objects could hardly have been the property of rural slaves. They may perhaps have found their way into the service quarters in redeposited earth.

9. Rostovtzeff SEHRE, p. 503 n. 21; Carrington, 1931, p. 116.

10. On upstairs storage: Varro, R.R., I.LVII.I ('granaria sublimia'); Pliny Ep. II. 17.13. ('horreum, sub hoc triclinium'), discussed by Sherwin-White, The letters of Pliny, Oxford 1966, p. 194ff.

11. cf. Palladius, Op.Ag. I.42.

12. Crova, Edilizia, p. 70.

13. K. D. White, 'Latifundia: a critical review of evidence on large estates in Italy and Sicily up to the end of the Ist century A.D.' Bull.Inst. Class. Stud. XIV (1967), p. 73.

14. Della Corte gives no indication of the function of rooms 14-17. Room 2 was a stable, for which see below, chapter VI.

15. The building possibly represents a partial excavation of a larger complex, with a courtyard to the south-west, onto which rooms 6-12 opened. It is therefore possible that the residential part of the farm building remains unexcavated. As it stands, however, the building can be interpreted as providing accommodation for a small work force of slaves.

16. On the press-rooms see chapter V.

17. C. F. Giuliani, Tibur—part II: Forma Italiae Reg. I. 3., Rome 1966, p. 75, following Gatti. No published record exists of the excavated contents of these rooms.

18. Della Corte, op.cit., p. 424; Pliny recommends the use of chestnut wood for vine-props (N.H. 17.147), as does Columella (D.R.R. 4.30. 2). For discussion see W. F. Jashemski, 'University of Maryland excavations at Pompeii', A.J.A. 74 (1970), p. 65; M. Bonnington, 'Trees, shrubs and plants as sources of raw materials' in White, F.E.R.W., p. 235ff.

19. A plan of the villa (unfortunately without a scale) appears in R. B. Bandinelli and M. Torelli, L'Arte dell'Antichità Classica 2: Etruria Roma, Turin 1976, no. 65; see also, Touring Club Italiano: Roma (7th ed.), Rome 1977, pp. 658-9.

20. Thus Bandinelli, op.cit.

CHAPTER V

PRESS-ROOMS

Renewed interest has recently been shown in the processes and apparatus used by the Romans in the production of olive oil and wine. However, since Drachmann's major study of the subject, more recent discussions have tended to concentrate either on the literary evidence, or on archaeological material from outside Italy.[1] The well-known passage in Cato (D.A. 18-19), in which he gives specifications for the construction of a large press-room, has received renewed criticism, but in this little mention has been made of the more recent archaeological material from Italy.[2] Yet throughout the Italian countryside, as the number of Roman farm sites that are identified and excavated continues to grow, the remains of numerous pressing installations have come to light. The importance of oil and wine production in Roman farming meant that many farms contained facilities for the processing of these products. Special press-rooms (torcularia) were built to house the apparatus required for the various processes of extraction and refining. However no comparative study has hitherto been attempted of the recorded remains of the many press-rooms that have been found at Italian sites. The scope of such a study is limited by the range of the surviving material; generally this is restricted to those parts of the pressing equipment which were constructed in durable materials and associated with the floor level of the press-room. However in the surviving pieces of equipment a considerable variety in design can be detected.

White, following Drachmann and basing his analysis on the literary evidence, divides Roman presses into five mechanical types: the lever-and-drum press, two types of lever-and-screw press, the firest screw press, and the 'congeries' press. The archaeological evidence can be less finely classified, owing mainly to the lack of survival of the wooden parts of the presses.[3] Nevertheless from the excavated press-rooms in Italy two distinctive types of lever press can be recognized.[4] These may be termed (i) platform presses, and (ii) circular-bed presses.

Platform presses are known from several Campanian sites, most notably from the press-rooms of the Villa Pisanella at Boscoreale and the Villa of The Mysteries at Pompeii.[5] The design is similar in each case; the press was mounted over an elevated platform, which was flanked by a raised curb to form a shallow basin, with its floor inclined to allow the extracted liquid to drain away into nearby receptacles. The mechanics of these presses is indicated by the square slots which held the vertical wooden beams of the press; one in the platform at the rear of the press to hold the main standard, and two in the press-room floor in front of the platform to hold the upright timbers of the winching drum. The beams were securely anchored by underground bolts or cross-pieces. Surviving examples of this type of press have generally been well recorded, and it is therefore on the next type of press that this chapter will concentrate.

The second type of press is known from many excavated remains in Italy, but has been poorly documented. The press is characterized by a circular press-bed, which is usually found in conjunction with a stone anchor block which served as a footing for the vertical beams at the rear of the press. Drachmann supposes that press remains of this type, consisting only of a rear anchor-stone and a press-bed, with no evidence for weightstones or drum supports, must indicate a type of lever-and-screw press, but such remains could also indicate the existence of a more simple manually controlled lever press. Although remains of this kind have been found at numerous Italian sites, standards of recording these have varied greatly. In some cases important details have been omitted, while in others there have been basic misinterpretations of the evidence and confusion of terminology.[6]

At most sites where press-rooms have been found the pavement surrounding the press base has been at least partially preserved. The platform presses usually occupied much of the room in which they were housed. The platforms themselves, over which the extracted liquid flowed, were customarily made of opus signinum, while at ground level the floor on which the operating personnel walked was more commonly simply one of trodden earth. With the circular-bed presses, however, the pavement around the base of the press, being at ground level, was simply the floor contained by the walls of the press-room. The most common material for the floor surface was again opus signinum.[7] Foundation materials have rarely been noted, except at Titignano where a rubble and mortar base beneath an opus signinum surface was recorded.[8] This would seem to correspond closely to the kind of pavement recommended for the press-room by Cato (D.A. 18.7). At other sites brick pavements have been found, with the bricks usually laid in the pattern of opus spicatum.[9] One press-room, at Granaraccio near Tivoli, had a pavement made of tufa paving stones, while at two sites pavements of monochrome mosaic were found. The latter could, however, be due to the conversion of domestic rooms to agricultural use.[10]

Set into the pavement at the rear of most excavated circular-bed presses was a rectangular stone block which acted as the footing for the upright timbers. Such blocks have been found at many sites and can be easily recognized by the two squared recesses cut into their upper surface, into which the uprights could be slotted. Surviving examples, made from tufa or travertine, range in length from 1.23-1.86 m, and in width from 0.37-0.74 m; the thickness of the blocks has not often been recorded (they have generally been left in situ), but, where noted, ranges from 0.15-0.53 m. The blocks may be related to Cato's forum (D.A. 18.3), which he describes as the footing for the rear uprights of the press and for which he gives measurements of 5 x 2.5 x 1.5 pedes (1.48 x 0.74 x 0.44 m). Cato also mentions the use of poured lead as a seal at the base of the timbers. At Granaraccio and Guidonia, near Rome, traces of lead were found around the inside edges of the recesses of the anchor-stones.[11]

The circular press-bed could be constructed in a number of different ways. In some cases it was a flat cylindrical slab of stone forming a small

FIG 14

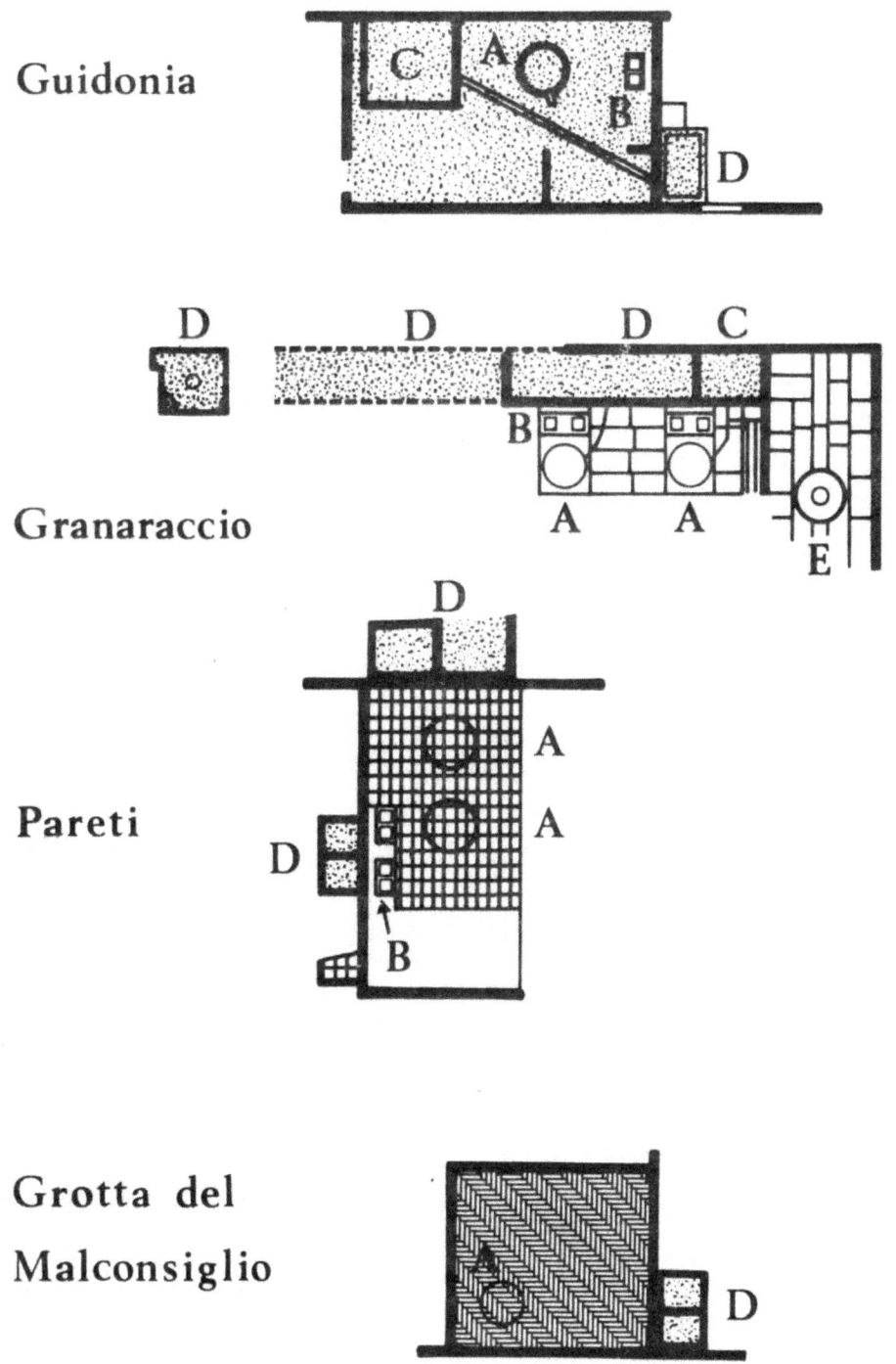

elevated platform; bases of this type have been found at Titignano and Guidonia. Elsewhere squared stones have been found with circular drainage grooves cut into their upper surface.[12] At Granaraccio a circular channel, 0.08 m wide, was cut into the flat surface formed by two contiguous blocks of tufa. Where the press-room pavement was made of brick, the press-bed was generally constructed in the same material, the bricks laid to form a circular footing, as at Pareti, Monte Canino and Grotta del Malconsiglio.

Different methods were employed for draining the extracted liquid away from the press-bed. Sometimes the entire pavement was inclined so that the liquid could run off in one direction.[13] Alternatively the press-bed was surrounded by a circular drainage channel, Cato's canalis rotunda (D.A. 18.6), and the liquid passed from this into a conduit which led to the collecting vats. The construction of such conduits varies in the surviving examples; at Guidonia it was built in brick with a mortar lining, whereas at Granaraccio a channel was cut into the tufa paving of the press-room floor.

For the initial extraction of the juice from grapes, treading tanks were commonly used. Often they were portable and made of wood, but at farms where wine production was carried out on a commercial scale more permanent types of tank are found.[14] At Granaraccio the base of a stone-built tank, measuring 2.25 x 1.40 m, and lined with opus signinum, was found close to one of the presses.[15] That this was a treading tank is clear from the fact that its floor was at a higher level than that of the press-room, and also was inclined so that the juice could run out through a hole at the base of the tank into a channel which joined the run-off duct leading from the press. Another large treading tank, 3.35 x 2.63 m, was excavated at Guidonia. This was brick built and lined with opus signinum. It was linked by means of a channel in the press-room floor with a collecting vat at a lower level.

Large sunken earthenware jars were sometimes placed immediately beside the press to receive the extracted liquid.[16] More commonly though, rectangular vats, used for the processing of olive oil, have been found located near the presses. The more elaborate plants preserve a series of three vats, designed so that the settling process which allowed the heavier lees to separate out of the oil, could be repeated more than once. The oil was either baled or passed by controlled overflow from one vat to the next.[17] Systems using three vats have been found at San Rocco (Francolise) and at Granaraccio. Often two adjacent vats were employed, or even a single vat with a central division. In some cases, as at Vicovaro and Scalea, a single vat sufficed.[18] Invariably the vats were lined with opus signinum. Sometimes steps are found built into one corner, presumably to facilitate the baling process, while at many sites the vats contain a circular sump in the middle of the floor, designed to serve as a catchment for the impurities as they sank to the bottom.[19]

Cato includes in the equipment to be housed in the press-room the mill used for bruising the olives prior to pressing (D.A. 18.5). The mechanics of the different types of Roman olive mills have been often discussed, most thoroughly by Drachmann.[20] However little comment has been made concerning the location of the mills in relation to the presses which they serviced. At only one site in Italy has a mill been found located, as Cato would wish, actually in the press-room itself. This was at a farm excavated near Stabiae, recorded by Ruggiero and discussed by Rich.[21] Here the mill was placed centrally between two platform presses. More commonly, however, mills were housed in a room adjacent to the press-room, in a sort of press-room annexe. This arrangement has been found at several farms; at the Villa Pisanella at Boscoreale, at Granaraccio, and possibly at a recently excavated farm at San Sebastiano al Vesuvio, where part of a mill was found 'fuori dell'ambiente E' (the press-room), and may have been located in a nearby or adjacent room.[22]

NOTES

1. A. G. Drachmann, Ancient Oil Mills and Presses, Copenhagen 1932. For recent discussion of the literary evidence see K. D. White, Farm Equipment of the Roman World, Cambridge 1975, pp. 107-17, 225-33; H. Plommer, Vitruvius and Later Roman Building Manuals, Cambridge 1973, pp. 8-11. On the archaeological evidence from the Roman provinces see, for example, H. Camps-Fabrer, L'olivier et l'huile dans l'Afrique Romaine, Alger 1953; D. Oates, 'The Tripolitanian Gebel: settlement of the Roman period around Gasr ed-Daun', P.B.S.R. XXI (1953), pp. 81-113; M. Ponsich, Recherches Archéologiques à Tanger et dans sa Région, Paris 1970, pp. 271-83; L. Maurin, 'Etablissement vinicole à Allas-les-Mines', Gallia XXII (1964), pp. 218-21; E. Catani, 'I frantoi della fattoria bizantina di El-Beida', Quaderni di archeologia della Libia 8 (1976), pp. 435-448.

2. J. Horle, Catos Hausbucher, Padeborn 1925, p. 177ff.; Drachmann, A.O.M.P., p. 99ff.; E. Jungst and P. Thielsher, 'Catos Keltern und Kollergange', Bonn. Jahrb. 154 (1954), pp. 32-93; R. Goujard, 'Etude critique de quelques passages de Caton, De Agricultura.' Rev. de Philologie 46.2 (1972), pp. 266-74; idem, Caton: De l'Agriculture, (Ed. Budé), Paris 1975.

3. White F.E.R.W., p. 229ff. Attempts to reconstruct press mechanisms from surviving archaeological remains have not been conclusive; for example the weightstones found at numerous Tripolitanian sites were interpreted by Drachmann, A.O.M.P. p. 97, as parts of lever and screw presses, but by Oates, op.cit., p. 86. Fig. 3, as parts of lever and drum presses.

4. Examples of direct screw presses have rarely been found in Italy. I know of only two sites at which press bases apparently belonging to this type of press have been found; at the Posto villa (Cat. 23), and at Luogosano, E. Gabrici, 'Luogosano—avanzi di costruzioni di età Romana sul Monte San Stefano', N.Sc. 1901, pp. 333-6.

5. Boscoreale Pisanella (Cat. 3); A. Maiuri, La Villa dei Misteri, Rome 1947, pp. 96-102. Other platform presses have been found at Stabiae (Cat. 34), in Pompeii, Ins. II.5 (W. F. Jashemsky, 'University of Maryland excavations at Pompeii, 1968', A.J.A. 74 (1970), pp. 62-7), and at another farm at Boscoreale (M. Della Corte, 'La villa rustica

N. Popidi Flori esplorata dalla signora Giovanna Zurlo-Pulzella nel fondo di sua proprietà in contrada Pisanella l'anno 1906', N.Sc. 1921, pp. 442-60.

6. For example the press-bed (ara) is referred to as a trapetum (mill) at Guidonia and Via Tiberina and as a mola (mill) at Titignano.

7. e.g. at Camerelle (Cat. 9), Guidonia (Cat. 11), Posta Crusta (Period II) (Cat. 22), Salapia (Cat. 29), Titignano (Cat. 35), and Via Tiberina (Cat. 38).

8. Minto (Cat. 35), p. 167.

9. E.g. at Grotta del Malconsiglio (Cat. 15), Posta Crusta (Period V) (Cat. 22), Vicovaro (Cat. 39), and Monte Canino (M. Pallotino, 'Capena—resti di costruzioni romane e medioevali in località "Montecanino"', N.Sc. 1937, pp. 7-28). At Pareti (Cat. 20) the bricks of the floor were laid in a simple block formation.

10. Tufa paving stones at Granaraccio (Cat. 14); mosaic at Scalea—fondo Marigliano-Filardi (Cat. 32) and at San Sebasteano al Vesuvio (Cat. 28).

11. Faccenna (Cat. 14), p. 152; Caprino (Cat. 11), p. 47.

12. E.g. at Orbetello, G. Maetzke, 'Orbetello—trovamenti archeologi vari', N.Sc. 1958, pp. 34-49 (dimensions: 51.5 x 38.5 x 0.21 m); at Tarquinia (Località San Giorgio), M. Pallotino, 'Tarquinia—rinvenimenti fortuiti nella necropoli e nel territorio, 1930-38', N.Sc. 1943, pp. 255-6 (dimensions: 1.77 x 1.70 x 0.40 m). This is the kind of press-bed found frequently in North Africa.

13. E.g. at Grotta del Malconsiglio and at Titignano.

14. White F.E.R.W., pp. 164-5. An elaborate treading-floor described by Palladius (Op.Ag. 1.18.1) is discussed by Plommer, op.cit., p. 8ff. and R. Martin, Palladius. Traité d'Agriculture (Livres I and II), Paris Paris (Les Belles Lettres) 1976, pp. 126-7.

15. Faccenna (Cat. 14), p. 151.

16. E.g. at Boscoreale Pisanella (Cat. 3) and Stabiae (Cat. 34).

17. White F.E.R.W., p. 159; Columella D.R.R. 12.52.11-12.

18. San Rocco (Cat. 27). The most common arrangement seems to be the two-vat system, found for example at Posto (Cat. 23), Guidonia, Grotta del Malconsiglio, Camerelle, Via Tiberina. The single vat with a central division recorded at Salapia (Cat. 29) may correspond to Columella's gemellar (D.R.R. 12.52.10); White F.E.R.W., pp. 149-50 s.v. gemellar, quotes another archaeiligical find, also from Apulia, which, he suggests, could exemplify Columella's device.

19. At a few sites, for example at Camerelle, Pareti and Grotta del Malconsiglio, large dolia were found standing in the settling vats. The reason for these is uncertain, though they may simply have been put in because the vats began to leak.

20. Drachmann A.O.M.P., pp. 7-49; cf. White F.E.R.W., pp. 226-9; R. J. Forbes, Studies in ancient technology III, Leiden 1955, pp. 146-8.

21. M. Ruggiero, Degli scavi di Stabia dal 1749 al 1782, Napoli 1881, p. 351ff.; A. Rich, A Dictionary of Roman and Greek Antiquity^2, New York 1901, s.v. 'torcularium'; Crova Edilizia, pp. 144-6; White F.E.R.W., s.v. 'lacus'.

22. G. C. Irelli, 'S. Sebastiano al Vesuvio—villa rustica romana', N.Sc. 1965, Suppl., p. 175.

Recorded remains of press-rooms in Italy:* Type II presses

Site	No. of presses	Dimensions of press-room	Pavement	Anchor-stone	Press-bed	
Camarelle (2) Cat.9.Fig.6	1	8.50 x 8.30 m	Op.Sig.		Op.Sig.	c.1.50 m diam.
Guidonia Cat. 11.Fig.14	1	5.8 x 3.8	Op.Sig.	Travertine 1.23 x 0.64 x 0.53	Travertine	1.86
Granaraccio Cat. 14.Fig.14	2		Tufa	Tufa, 1.86 x 0.74	Tufa	1.50
Grotta del Malconsiglio. Cat. 15.Fig.14	1	7.0 x 6.6	Brick		Brick	1.60
Monte Canino, Appendix B	1	6.3 x 4.7	Brick	Travertine	Brick	
Pareti, Cat. 20. Fig.14	3		Brick		Brick	1.80
Posta Crusta (Period II) Cat. 22. Fig.2, 9	1	3.5 x 3.1	Op.Sig.			
Posta Crusta (Period V)	1	12.3 x 4.2	Brick		Brick	c.1.70
San Sebasteano al Vesuvio Cat. 28.			Mosaic	Travertine 1.35 x 0.55		
Scalea-fondo Marigliano-Filardi Cat. 32	1		Mosaic	Tufa 1.50 x 0.54 x 0.26		
Scalea-fondo di Puglia Cat.32.	1		Op.Sig.	Tufa 1.37 x 0.37 x 0.15		
Titignano Cat. 35.	1	5.40 x 2.70	Op.Sig.	Travertine 1.30 x 0.60	Travertine	1.30
Via Tiberina Cat. 38.	1	9.30 x 5.80	a) Brick b) Op.Sig.			1.80
Vicovaro (3) Cat. 39.Fig. 13b	1		Op.Sig			1.15

* This list does not include the numerous sites at which random finds of a single piece of press-room equipment have occurred.

CHAPTER VI

GRANARIES, STORE-ROOMS AND CATTLE SHEDS

The function which the individual rooms of a farm served is not always precisely defined by excavation. Some clue to the use to which different rooms were put may be provided by an analysis of the excavated contents. But perhaps the clearest indication exists in the case of farm facilities which, for a specific function, required particular features in their design.[1] This has already been illustrated with respect to facilities built for the processing of olive oil and wine. Distinctive structural elements can also help in identifying rooms used as granaries, store-rooms and cattle sheds.

Granaries

Rickman's study of Roman public granaries in the northern provinces of the empire has provided a synoptic account of building types in that area.[2] The North European climate made it imperative that the floors of granaries be raised above ground level. This could be done in a number of different ways, either by setting the floor on a series of dwarf piers, rather in the manner of a hypocaust, or by raising it on a number of transverse or longitudinal sleeper beams.[3] In a small granary the floor could also be raised by laying it on a masonry offset parallel to the wall, as is seen in the Roman villa at Stroud (Hampshire) in England.[4] Both Columella and Vitruvius emphasize the need for a granary, even in a Mediterranean climate, to have an elevated, and hence well ventilated floor.[5] Columella gives details of the way in which the ground beneath may be treated to prevent the intrusion of vermin. He suggests covering the earth with a layer of opus signinum and sealing this against the side walls of the room at ground level. Neither author, however, gives details of how the floor of the granary is to be supported.

Facilities at only two farm sites in Italy can be identified with certainty as granaries. One of these is a room in a farm building at Vicovaro (Fig. 13b, 2), the other at Russi (Fig. 9, 6). Neither of these granaries was built at a distance from the rest of the farm, as Vitruvius advises (D.A. VI.6.5), but each formed part of a larger complex of rooms. The granary at Vicovaro was a large room measuring 29.5 x 14.8 m with walls in reticulate. The interior of the room contained a triple series of dwarf piers, whose purpose, it would seem, was to support an elevated platform. The space between the piers is transversely 3.0 m and longitudinally 2.8 m. The large dimensions of the granary would seem to suggest that the estate for which it existed was extensive.[6]

At Russi a smaller granary, measuring 7 x 9.9 m, flanked the main entrance to the south courtyard. This room contained two series of dwarf

FIG 15

Store-rooms   Scale 1:500

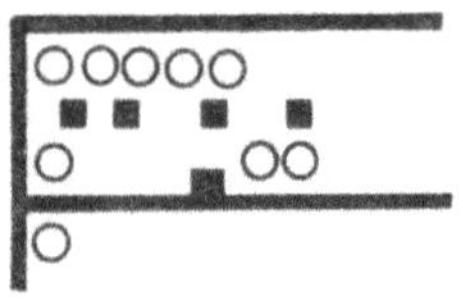

A Casalotto

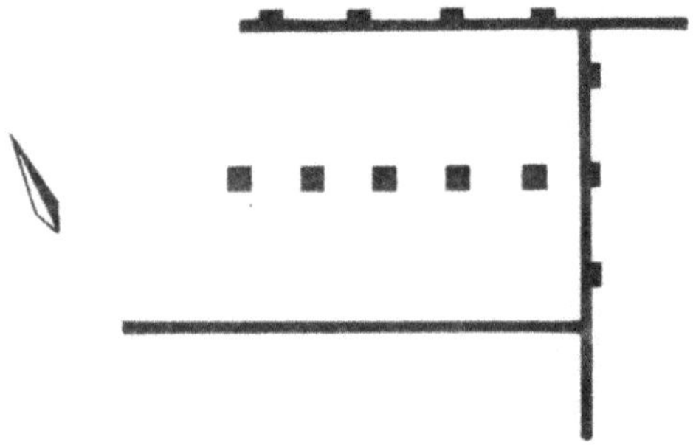

B Pratella

Cattle-sheds

C Lucinico

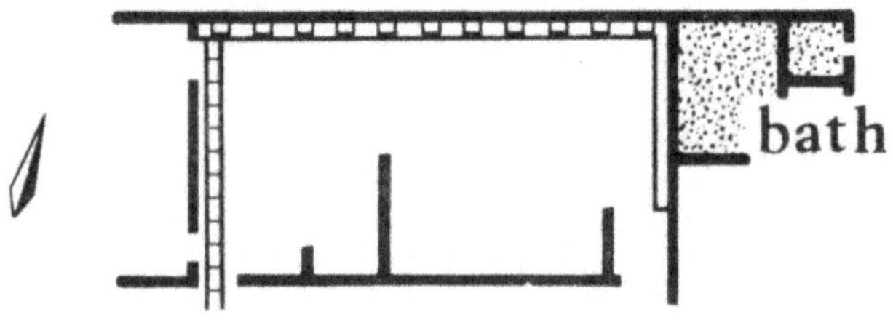

bath

D Monte Irsi

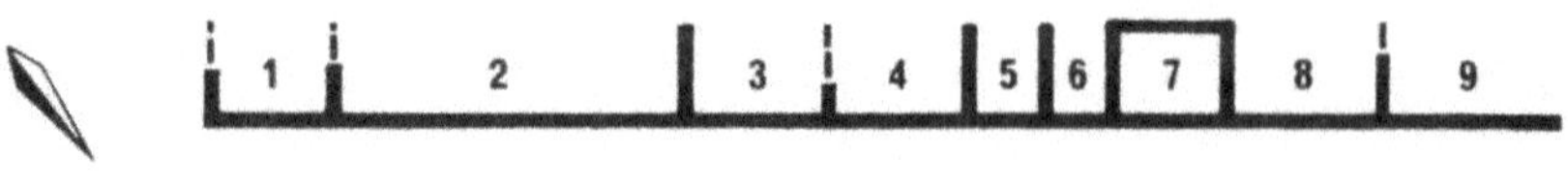

1 2 3 4 5 6 7 8 9

piers, arranged in double lines along each side of the room. The distance between the rows is approximately 0.60 m, while each pair of piers is longitudinally about 2.50 m apart. A central aisle, 3.0 m wide, separated the two series of piers. The piers were constructed using flat tiles superimposed on a base of mortared brick rubble. Most probably they would have supported a wooden superstructure designed to provide for the dry storage of grain. The granary would thus have contained two rows of bins ranged along each side of a central aisle. The location of the granary, flanking the main entrance and with access directly into the courtyard, allowed for easy loading and unloading of supplies.

The large barn at Russi (Fig. 9, 1) may also have contained grain bins along its western side. In this room two different series of internal piers, both made of brick, were identified. The larger of these probably served as roof supports. The secondary series of smaller piers along the west wall of the room (Fig. 9, 2) may on the other hand have supported a raised platform with storage bins. The piers here are 2.0 m apart longitudinally, only slightly closer than those in the two granaries discussed above. The presence of what appears to be an oil settling tank in the south-east corner of the barn indicates another aspect of the farm's economy.

Store-rooms

A few farms in Italy include in their plans long store-rooms which, although they were probably used for storing a variety of products and equipment, can be considered here as a group, owing to their similarity of design. These rooms characteristically have a long rectangular form, with a single row of piers down the centre to serve as bases for the upright timbers which held the wooden framework of the roof. In some cases, for example at Casalotto (Cat. 8. Fig. 16a) and Pratella (Cat. 24. Fig. 16b), the roof supports rested on a series of closely spaced piers. At the Villa Selvasecca (Fig. 3a, s) the two surviving base-blocks probably formed part of a series running centrally down the long axis of the store-room. Elsewhere the internal support for the roof was limited to two widely spaced piers. This arrangement is seen in the store-room of the Boscoreale Stazione farm (Fig. 4b, 6) and may also have existed in the long room to the south of the Villa of Publius Fannius Sinistor at Boscoreale (Fig. 7b, 4) and in the outbuilding at Monna Felice (Cat. 17). Different materials and modes of construction were employed to make the piers in these various store-rooms. At Pratella they were formed by packing small squared stones around a rubble core. At Casalotto the piers were built of mortared brick, while at the Villa Selvasecca squared tufa blocks were used.

The use to which these rooms were put doubtless varied from site to site. Storage of farm produce and equipment seems a likely function. Certainly this was the case at Casalotto, where the room was found to contain numerous sunken dolia, and clearly served as a store-room for wine or oil.[8] The store-room of the Boscoreale Stazione farm seems to have served a double function, both as a store for wood and hay and as a stable.[9] The dimensions of the various store-rooms correspond as follows (dimensions in metres):

Site	External measurements	Intercolumnar space
Boscoreale Stazione	21.8 x 5.8	6.3
Boscoreale (Villa of Publius Fannius Sinistor)	x 6.3	
Casalotto	x 5.1	2.20-2.50
Monna Felice	16+ x 3.2+	
Pratella	x 13.5	2.10-2.30
Selvasecca	28.5 x 6.0	2.70

Cattle-sheds

Facilities for sheltering cattle have sometimes been identified in excavated farm buildings in Italy. At Gragnano (Cat. 12) one of the larger rooms (Fig. 13b, 2) was found to contain the skeletal remains of a number of oxen and horses. At the time of the eruption, therefore, it was certainly being used as a shelter for livestock and it seems possible that this was the regular function of the room. A good example of this kind of facility has been found in a partially explored farm building at Lucinico in Venezia Giulia (Cat. 17. Fig. 16c). The function of the large room here is strongly suggested by its internal features and its location. Along the north wall of the room ran a water trough which was bridged at regular intervals by horizontal slabs of stone, leaving a series of openings approximately 1.30 m apart. These openings would conveniently have allowed for the watering of a dozen animals. The room was located next to the farm's bath rooms and could thereby benefit from the warmth of the latter's heating system. For the same reason Vitruvius (D.A. VI. 6.1) recommends that the cattle-shed should be located next to the farm's kitchen. The excavated contents of the room at Lucinico included numerous animal bones of which a high proportion were from oxen; their presence can be accounted for by the fact that the building was destroyed by a sudden fire.[10]

Oxen were generally stalled in pairs. An indication of the size of stall required for this purpose is given in several of the literary sources. Vitruvius (D.A. VI.6.2) recommends a width of 10-15 pedes (2.96-4.44 m) per stall. Columella (D.R.R. 1.6.6) suggests a slightly narrower stall measuring 2.66-2.96 m in width. According to Vitruvius the depth of the stall should be at least 2.07 m. The considerable width of the room at Gragnano (6.0 m) suggests that it contained a double series of stalls, perhaps providing for the stabling of oxen on one side of a central aisle and horses on the other.[11] The measurements given by the literary sources have helped to interpret a farm building found at Monte Irsi in Basilicata (Cat. 19. Fig. 16d). The building here, constructed in the mid 2nd century B.C., consisted of a long series of open-ended rooms. The walls were roughly built of earth-bonded sandstone slabs and most of the rooms had a trodden earth floor. The building was probably covered by a simple sloping tiled roof and its general character suggested that it was an agricultural out-building of some kind.[12] The dimensions of the rooms (3.5-5.25 m in width, 3.25-3.5 m in depth) led to the conclusion that they were probably stalls for cattle, while the small enclosed room (room 7) was used by the herdsman.[13]

Another building which may have provided shelter for livestock is the portico along the north-west side of the courtyard of the Posto farm (period I) at Francolise (Cat. 23. Fig. 4a, 4). This had a depth of 3.6 m and the space between the supports ranged from 2.3-3.2 m, probably allowing for a double stalling of oxen between each.

The dimensions of the different excavated cattle-sheds correspond as follows (dimensions in metres);

Site	Dimensions of cattle-shed	Width of stall
Gragnano	13.0 x 6.0	
Lucinico	21.0 x 10.85	1.3 (single)
Monte Irsi	55+ x 3.25-3.5	3.5-5.3 (double)
Posto	16.8+ x 3.6	2.3-3.2 (double)

NOTES

1. S. Applebaum, 'Farms and their uses', in H. P. Finberg (ed), The Agrarian History of England and Wales: Vol. I, Cambridge 1972, p. 151ff.

2. G. Rickman, Roman Granaries and Store-buildings, Cambridge 1971. cf. A. P. Gentry, Roman Military Stone-built Granaries in Britain, Oxford 1976; White R.F., pp. 189, 427-8.

3. Rickman Granaries, p. 213ff. In Britain only four stone granaries have floors raised on dwarf piers. These are at Housesteads, South Shields, Castlecary and Ribchester. The rest employ sleeper beams. In Germany, however, the preference is reversed.

4. Applebaum, op.cit., p. 175.

5. Columella D.R.R. I.6. 12f. Vitruvius D.A. VI.6.4. The text of Vitruvius is here corrupt. The editor of the Loeb text prefers the reading sublinata, a word meaning 'smeared' (from the verb lino). However, the reading sublimata, meaning 'elevated', seems more appropriate in the context.

6. The width of the granary (14.8 m) far exceeds the average width of public granaries in northern Europe, which is around 6.09 m. Rickman Granaries, p. 228.

7. The granary was excavated in 1969; for details see D. Scagliarini, 'La Villa Romana di Russi' in G. C. Susini, La Villa Romana, Faenza 1971, pp. 123-4.

8. On store-rooms containing sunken dolia, see Rickman Granaries, pp. 73-6.

9. Crova Edilizia, p. 45.

10. S. Stucchi, 'Lucinico (Gorizia)—villa rustica romana', N.Sc. 1950, pp. 8.16.

11. Applebaum, op.cit., p. 149.

12. A. M. Small, Monte Irsi, Southern Italy, (B.A.R. Supp. Vol. 36), Oxford, 1977, pp. 44-7, Figs. 8 and 9.

13. Small, ibid., pp. 47-8.

CHAPTER VII

CHRONOLOGY

At only a few of the sites discussed in this volume has the complex structural history of the farm buildings been accurately determined by a careful analysis of the excavated dating evidence. Despite the small number of such sites, however, a comparative study of their dating evidence may provide some tentative clues to the chronological development of rural construction in Italy.[1]

The original construction of a number of the farms can be dated to the 2nd century B.C. (Cat. 20.23.26.33.41). The buildings datable to this century are generally of modest proportions and for the most part remained in their original form throughout the following century.[2] A few of the Campanian farms in the region of Vesuvius may also have been built in the later 2nd century B.C. (Cat. 3) although construction of the majority has been placed somewhere in the 1st century B.C.[3] During the 1st century B.C. there is evidence for considerable building activity elsewhere in rural Italy, including the initial construction of a number of larger farmhouses and villas (Cat. 9.25.27.38) which, even in their early phases, can probably be associated with sizeable estates.

During the 1st century A.D. several of the farms examined underwent extensive and elaborate reconstruction (Cat. 15.23.27.41) and there may at this time have been a corresponding increase in the size of the farms' land holdings. Surface material suggests that construction of the very large 'fragmented' villas discussed in chapter III (Cat. 7.10.40) should also be dated to the early Imperial period. These villas too can probably be associated with large estates whose creation may have involved the absorbtion of some smaller properties. It is interesting to note that, by the end of the 1st century A.D., only one (Cat. 18) of the small farmsteads discussed in chapter 1 appears still to have been occupied in its original form; the others had by this time either been enlarged (Cat. 23) or abandoned (Cat. ?22.26.33).

While occupation of many farms and villas is attested during the 2nd century A.D. (Cat. 7.9.16.18.20.23.25.27.40.41) new building during this period appears limited. There is, however, evidence for reconstruction at some of the larger villas (Cat. 25.40). Again during the 3rd century A.D., although there is further evidence for occupation at many sites (Cat. 7.9.16.20.22.23.25.40.41), there is little firm evidence for rebuilding at any of these sites.[4] The subsequent history of the buildings is often far from certain. In a number of cases life at the farms seems to have ceased at some point during the 4th century (Cat. 7.22.25.41). Evidence for the continuation of rural settlement beyond the 4th century A.D. has been accumulated in regional surveys in different parts of Italy but the detailed history of individual farm buildings in late antiquity has rarely been deciphered.[5] Some farms, like that at Monte Canino in the Ager Capenas, would seem eventually to have become associated with new ecclesiastical buildings;[6] while elsewhere it is possible that some rural properties may have developed into the type of defensible stronghold for which there is some evidence from the Roman provinces in late antiquity.[7]

From the chronology of the different farms that have been discussed it is possible to make some comment on the development of rural architecture in Italy. We have noted earlier (above pp. 22-6) how, at least by the age of Augustus, certain design features common in Roman domestic architecture—axial planning, the developed atrium, elegant peristyles—were being employed in the construction of rural buildings. The farm buildings of the early Imperial period reveal the extent to which this trend continued. Many of the farmhouses and villas built or rebuilt during the 1st century A.D. were designed with refined architectural features; buildings were constructed with elegant peristyles and colonnades (Cat. 27), atria (Cat. 13.41) and elaborate bath rooms (Cat. 23.27). At the same time the surface remains of a small number of very large early Imperial villas (Cat.7.10.40) testify to the existence of a looser type of villa planning in which certain of the villas' facilities, in particular the bath rooms, were located in separate and independent buildings. The rural villas at Russi (Cat. 25) provides further evidence for luxury and fragmentation in villa architecture of the 2nd century A.D. Also during the 1st and 2nd centuries A.D. more sophisticated agricultural facilities appear at many sites; a screw press was installed at Posto (Cat. 23); stone granaries were built at Russi and Vicovaro (Cat. 25.30);[8] an irrigated cattle-shed was constructed at Lucinico (Cat. 16). There is at present little evidence for architectural innovation in the construction of farm buildings in Italy after the 2nd century A.D. This picture may, however, be altered by further excavation.[9]

NOTES

1. The non-stratigraphic excavations in the nineteenth century and the early part of this century of the so-called "Campanian villae rusticae" did not produce a reliable chronology for these sites. While life at the farms came to an abrupt end in 79 A.D., the early history of the individual buildings is generally obscure. An attempt to date some of the farms on the recorded evidence of wall paintings and construction materials was made by Carrington, 1931 pp. 125-9. The more recently excavated farm at San Sebastiano al Vesuvio (Cat. 28) has produced evidence for reoccupation after the eruption of 79 A.D., but this building, which is located to the north-west of the mountain, evidently escaped the worst of the volcanic deposits which destroyed the farms to the south (see map II); G. Irelli, N.Sc. 1965 (Supp.), p. 161ff.

2. Only at Posto (Cat. 23) is there evidence for major rebuilding during the 1st century B.C.

3. Carrington 1931, pp. 125-9; G. Lugli, La tecnica edilizia romana (2 vols.), Rome 1957, pp. 426, 505.

4. The construction of a road, for which there is epigraphic evidence (see above, chapter III note 4) at Villa Magna (Cat. 40) may have been associated with other building activity at the site in the early 3rd century A.D.

5. Regional studies of rural settlement in late antiquity include; G. B. D. Jones, op.cit. (1963), pp. 134-5; A. Kahane, L. M. Threipland and J. B. Ward-Perkins, op.cit. (1968), pp. 152-3; L. Ruggini, Economia e Società nell' "Italia annonaria", Milan 1961, pp. 527-30.

6. Jones, op.cit. (1962), p. 162.

7. For a discussion of the evidence for fortified villas in the Roman provinces in late antiquity see Ward-Perkins, E.R.A., pp. 526-7; M. Cagiano de Azevedo, 'Ville rustiche tardoantiche e installazioni agricole altomedievali' Settimane di Spoleto XIII (1966), pp. 663-94. Of particular interest is a type of fortified villa with a frontal colonnade and corner towers; this architectural type is depicted on a well-known 4th century mosaic from Carthage (Bardo Museum, Room X. A7) and is reflected in the architecture of the 4th century Imperial palace at Split in Yugoslavia. Cagiano de Azevedo points to the same architectural type recurring in the 5th/6th century villa at Meleda (Mljet) in Yugoslavia, and in the 6th century 'Villa of Theodoric' at Ravenna.

8. The reticulate walls of the Vicovaro granary suggest a late Republican or early Imperial date for the building; G. Lugli, M.A. XXXI (1926) p. 126.

9. For example by the current University of Alberta excavations of a late Roman farmhouse at San Giovanni di Ruoti in Basilicata; for an interim report of the first season's finds, see A. M. Small and R. J. Buck, 'San Giovanni di Ruoti, Southern Italy (1977)' Classical News and Views XXII.I (Jan. 1978), pp. 5-8; a report of the second season's finds is forthcoming in C.N.V. XXIII (1979).

Map I Map showing the location of the farm buildings listed in Appendix A

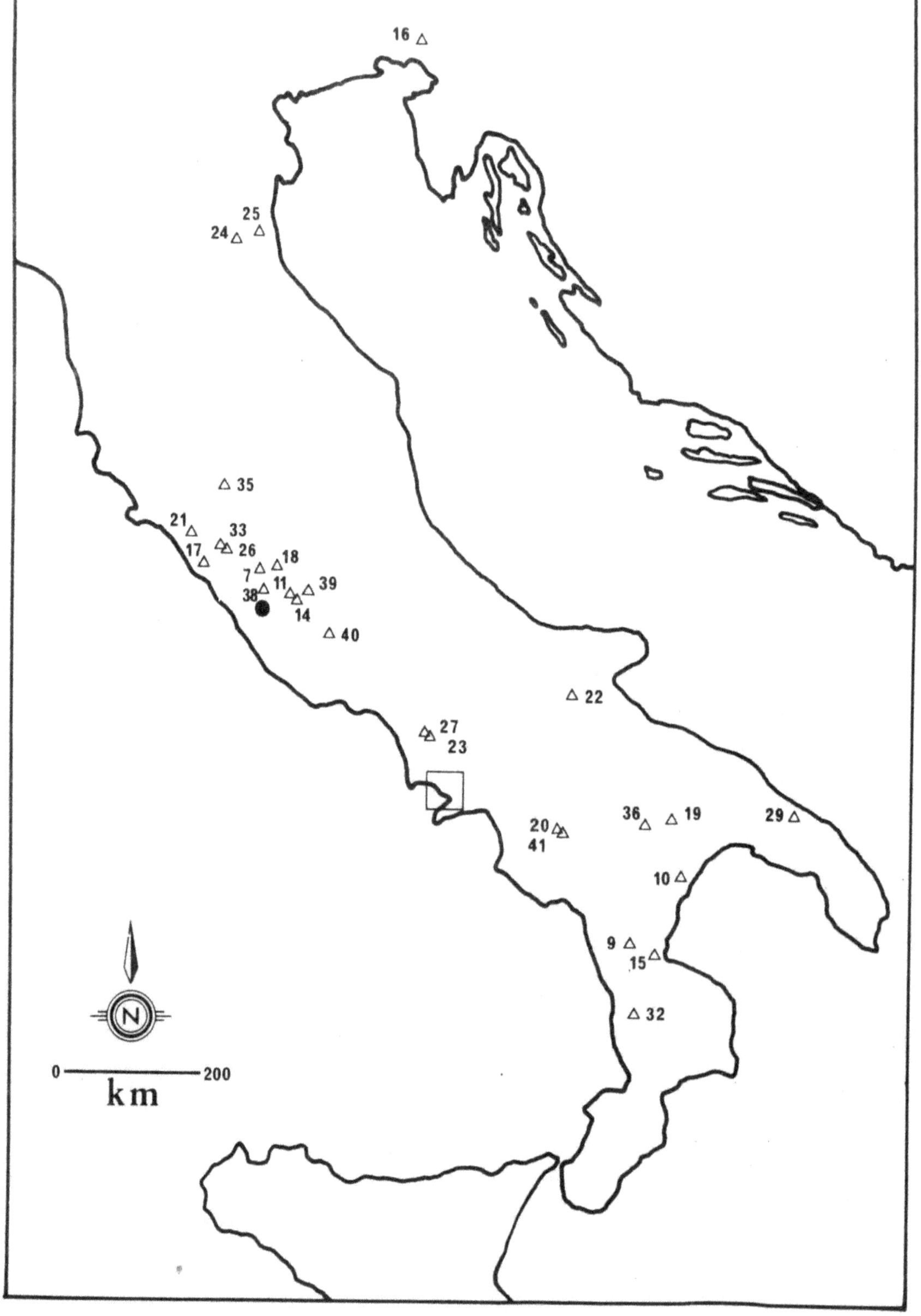

APPENDIX A

An alphabetical catalogue of farm buildings discussed in the text, with bibliographical references.

1. Boscoreale (contrada Civitá Giuliana), Campania:
   A. Sogliano, N.Sc. 1895, p. 214, N.Sc. 1897, p. 391; Crova, Edilizia, p. 77, Fig. 9; Rostovtzeff SEHRE, p. 552 No. 14.

2. Boscoreale (contrada Civitá Giuliana), Campania:
   M. Della Corte, 'Altra villa rustica, scavata dal sig. cav. Carlo Rossi-Filangieri nel fondo di Raffaele Brancaccio, nella stessa contrada Civita Giuliana (comune di Boscoreale) nei mesi da gennaio a marzo 1904', N.Sc. 1921, pp. 423-6; Carrington, 1931, p. 122; Crova, Edilizia, pp. 177-8; Rostovtzeff SEHRE, p. 552 No. 26.

3. Boscoreale (Pisanella), Campania:
   For the excavation see A. Pasqui, 'La villa Pompeiana della Pisanella presso Boscoreale', M.A. VII (1897), pp. 397-554; G. Fiorelli, N.Sc. 1876, p. 196, N.Sc. 1877, p. 17, 96, 128; A. Sogliano, N.Sc. 1895, p. 207; A. Pasqui, N.Sc. 1896, p. 234. For the treasure from the villa, now in the Louvre, see A.H. de Villefosse, 'Le tresor de Boscoreale', Monuments Piot V (1899), p. 7ff. For comment Cagnat and Chapot, Manuel d'Archeologie Romaine, Paris 1916, pp. 302-6; Carrington, 1931, p. 119; idem, Pompeii, p. 89f; Crova, Edilizia, pp. 47-54; J. Day, 'Agriculture in the life of Pompeii', Yale Classical Studies III (1932), pp. 180-4; Frank ESAR V, p. 172, p. 264ff; Rostovtzeff SEHRE, p. 552 No. 13, p. 564; J.E. Skydsgaard, Den Romerske Villa Rustica, Copenhagen 1961, p. 12f; C.A. Yeo, 'The economics of Roman and American Slavery', Finanzarchiv XIII (1952), p. 445ff; White, R.F., p. 422ff.

4. Boscoreale (Stazione), Campania:
   M. Della Corte, 'Villa Rustica, esplorata dal sig. Ferruccio De Prisco nel fondo d'Acunzo, posto immediatamente a mezzogiorno del piazzale della stazione ferroviaria di Boscoreale (Ferrovia dello Stato), l'anno 1903', N.Sc. 1921, pp. 436-42; Crova, Edilizia, p. 43f, Fig. 1; Rostovtzeff SEHRE, p. 552 No. 28; Day, op.cit., pp. 167-208; Carrington, 1931, pp. 116-22; White, 1970, p. 430, Fig. 7.

5. Boscoreale (Villa of Publius Fannius Sinistor), Campania:
   F. Barnabei, La villa pompeiana di P. Fannio Sinistore, Rome 1901; P. Lehmann, Roman Wall Paintings from Boscoreale, Cambridge, Mass. 1951; Rostovtzeff SEHRE, p. 552 No. 26; M. Robertson, 'The Bsocoreale figure paintings', JRS XLV (1955), pp. 58-67.

6. Boscotrecase (Villa of Tiberius Claudius Eutuchus), Campania:
M. Della Corte, 'La villa rustica "Ti. Claudi. Eutychi, Caesaris l(iberti)" esplorata dal sig. cav. Ernesto Santini, nel fondo della sua proprietà alla contrada Rota (Comune di Boscotrecase), negli anni 1903-5', N.Sc. 1922, pp. 459-79; Carrington, 1931, p. 112; idem, 1934, p. 273; Day, op.cit., p. 176; Crova, Edilizia, p. 68, Fig. 7; Rostovtzeff SEHRE, p. 552 No. 31.

7. Casalaccio (Ager Veientanus), Lazio:
A. Kahane, L.M. Threipland, J.B. Ward-Perkins, 'The Ager Veientanus North and East of Rome', P.B.S.R. XXIII (1968), sites 540-541, pp. 139-44, 157.

8. Casalotto (Via Cornelia), Lazio:
P. Romanelli, 'Via Cornelia - resti di villa rustica', N.Sc. 1933, pp. 246-8.

9. Castrovillari (contrada Camerelle), Calabria:
F.T. Bertocchi, 'La villa Romana di Camerelle', Klearchos V (1963), pp. 135-152; C. Pepe, Memorie storiche della città di Castrovillari, (1880), p. 64.

10. Cugno dei Vagni* (Siris/Heraclea), Basilicata:
M. Lacava, Topographia e Storia di Metaponto, Napoli 1891, pp. 17-20; L. Quilici, Forma Italiae, Regio III Vol. I: Siris - Heraclea, Rome 1967, pp. 123-132; D. Adamesteanu, La Basilicata Antica, Rome 1975 p. 224f. Quilici refers to the site by the name Ciglio dei Vagni.

11. Guidonia (aeroporto di), Roma:
C. Caprino (Guidonia - villa rustica con torcularium' N.Sc. 1944-5 pp. 39-51.

12. Gragnano (contrada Carità), Campania:
M. Della Corte, 'Villa rustica esplorata dal sig. cav. Carlo Rossi - Filangieri in un fondo del sig. comm. Agnello Marchetti, posto immediatamente ad ovest della Via Scafati - Gragnano, nella contrada Carità, in comune di Gragnano', N.Sc. 1923, pp. 275-80; Carrington, 1931, p. 122; idem, 1934, p. 272; Crova, Edilizia, pp. 70-2; Day, op.cit., p. 185; Rostovtzeff SEHRE, p. 553 No. 34; White RF, pp. 437-8; Yeo, op.cit., pp. 449-51.

13. Gragnano (contrada Messigno), Campania:
M. Della Corte, 'Villa rustica esplorata dal sig. Giacomo Matrone in un fondo di sua proprietà, posto immediatamente ad Occidente della via vicinale che attraversa, in direzione Nord - Sud, la contrada Messigno, in comune di Gragnano', N.Sc. 1923, pp. 271-4; Carrington, 1931, p. 121; idem., 1934, p. 275; idem., 1936, pp. 94-5; Rostovtzeff SEHRE, p. 553 No. 33.

14. Grannaracio (Tivoli), Lazio:
D. Faccenna, 'Tivoli (Localita Grannaracio) - resti della parte rustica di una villa', N.Sc. 1957, pp. 148-53.

15. Grotta del Malconsiglio (Sybaris), Calabria:
E. Galli, 'Due ville romane in agro Sybaritano', Atti del IInd Congresso

nazionale di studi romani: I, Rome 1931, p. 267f.; idem., 'La villa rustica della Grotta del Malconsiglio', A.M.S.M.G. 1929, p. 46f; E. Magaldi, Lucania Romana Rome 1947, pp. 62-3.

16. Lucinico (Gorizia), Venezia Giulia:
S. Stucchi, 'Lucinico (Gorizia) - villa rustica romana', N.Sc. 1950, pp. 1-16.

17. Monna Felice (Civitavecchia), Lazio:
O. Toti, 'Civitavecchia - edificio rustico romano in località Monna Felice', N.Sc. 1966, pp. 79-90; M. Torelli, 'Contributo dell'archeologia alla storia sociale: 1 - 1 'Etruria e l'Apulia', in Dialoghi di Archeologia, Anno IV-V (1970-1), pp. 431-442.

18. Monte Forco (Ager Capenas), Lazio:
G.D.B. Jones, 'Capena and the Ager Capenas: Part 1', P.B.S.R. XVII (1962), pp. 172-3, site No. 154; idem., P.B.S.R. XVIII (1963), pp. 147-58.

19. Monte Irsi (Irsina), Basilicata:
A.M. Small, Monte Irsi, Southern Italy, (B.A.R. Supp. Vol. 36), Oxford, 1977, pp. 44-48.

20. Pareti (Buccino), Campania:
S.L. Dyson, 'Excavations at Buccino, 1971', A.J.A. 76 (1972), pp. 161-3.

21. Portaccia (Tarquinia), Lazio:
P. Romanelli, 'Tarquinia - rinvenimenti fortuiti nella necropoli e nel territorio (1930-38)', N.Sc. 1943, pp. 213-261.

22. Posta Crusta (Foggia), Puglia:
G. De Boe, 'Villa romana in località "Posta Crusta", Rapporto provisorio sulle campagne di scavo 1972 e 1973', N.Sc. 1975, pp. 516-30; J. Mertens, Ordona V, pp. 19-22.

23. Posto (Francolise), Campania:
P. Von Blankenhagen, M.A. Cotton, J.B. Ward-Perkins, 'Two Roman villas at Francolise', P.B.S.R. XX (1965), pp. 55-69; idem., 'Francolise (Caserta) - Rapporto provisorio del 1962-4 sugli scavi di due ville romane della Repubblica e del Primo Impero', N.Sc. 1965, pp. 237-252.

24. Pratella (Imola), Emilia e Romagna:
D. Scagliarini, Ravenna e le ville romane in Romagna, (Collana di quaderni di antichità Ravennati, cristiane e bizantine diretta dal prof. G. Bovini dell'Università di Bologna. Quaderno No. X), Ravenna 1968, pp. 16-21, Fig. 10; G.A. Mansuelli, 'La villa romana nell'Italia settentrionale', P.P. LVII (1957), pp. 454-55.

25. Russi (Ravenna), Emilia e Romagna:
G.A. Mansuelli, La villa romana di Russi, Faenza, 1962; idem., 'Russi (Ravenna) - scavo di una villa romana (1953-5)', Bolletino d'Arte II (1956), pp. 151-57; idem., Le ville del mondo Romano, Milano 1958, pp. 77-8; D. Scagliarini, op.cit., pp. 12-28; idem.,

'La villa romana di Russi (Ravenna): Campagna di Scavo 1969' in G. Susini (ed.), La Villa Romana, Faenza 1971, pp. 117-142.

G. Montanari et al., Russi: la villa romana, la città, Faenza 1975.

26. Sambuco (Blera), Lazio:
C. Ostenberg, 'Luni and Villa Sambuco', in Etruscan Culture, Land and People, Malmo 1960, pp. 313-20; E. Berggren, 'A new approach to the closing centuries of Etruscan history', Arctos V (1967), pp. 29-43.

27. San Rocco (Francolise), Campania:
P. Von Blankenhagen, M.A. Cotton, J.B. Ward-Perkins, 'Two Roman villas at Francolise', P.B.S.R. XX (1965), pp. 55-69, idem., 'Francolise (Caserta) - Rapporto provvisorio del 1962-4 sugli scavi di due ville romane della Repubblica e del Primo Impero', N.Sc. 1965, pp. 237-252, J.B. Ward-Perkins, E.R.A., p. 319, Fig. 124.

28. San Sebastiano al Vesuvio, Campania:
G.C. Irelli, 'S. Sebastiano al Vesuvio - villa rustica romana', N.Sc. 1965, Suppl., pp. 161-178.

29. San Vito (Salapia), Puglia:
M.D. Marin, 'Scavi archeologici nella contrada S. Vito presso il lago di Salpi', Archivio Storico Pugliese 1964, p. 171ff.

30. Scafati (contrada Crapolla), Campania:
M. Della Corte, 'Villa rustica parzialmente esplorata dall' on. sig. Vincenzo De Prisco in un fondo di sua proprietà alla contrada Crapolla (comune di Scafati)', N.Sc. 1923, pp. 284-7; Rostovtzeff SEHRE, P. 553 No. 36.

31. Scafati (contrada Spinelli), Campania:
M. Della Corte, 'Villa rustica scavata dal sig. ing. Gennaro Matrone in un fondo di sua proprietà situato nella contrada Spinelli (comune di Scafati) a sud del portellone n. 27 nel R. Canale del Sarno', N.Sc. 1923. pp. 280-284; Rostovtzeff SEHRE, p. 553 No. 35: Skydsgaard, Den Romerske Villa Rustica, Copenhagen 1961, p. 17f., Fig. 7.

32. Scalea (Cosenza), Calabria:
G. Pesce, 'Scalea - trovamenti varii', N.Sc. 1936, pp. 67-74.

33. Selvasecca (Blera), Lazio:
E. Berggren and A. Andren, 'Blera (località Selvasecca)—Villa rustica etrusco-romana con manifattura di terracotte architettoniche', N.Sc. 1969, pp. 51-71; Berggren, 'A new approach to the closing centuries of Etruscan history, Arctos V (1967), pp. 29-43.

34. Stabiae/Gragnano, Campania:
M. Ruggiero, Degli scavi di Stabia dal 1794 at 1782, Naples 1881, p. 351ff; A. Rich, A Dictionary of Roman and Greek Antiquity,[2] New York 1901, s.v. 'torcularium'.

35. Titignano (comune di Orvieto), Umbria:
A. Minto, 'Titignano (frazione del comune di Orvieto) - avanzi di un torcularium di età romana', N.Sc. 1914, pp. 167-8.

36. Tolve - Moltone (Tolve), Basilicata:
    G. Tocca, 'L'attività archeologica nella Basilicata settentrionale',
    in Atti del XIII convegno di studi sulla Magna Grecia, Napoli 1974,
    pp. 461-7. Plates 102-5; D. Adamesteanu, La Basilicata Antica,
    Rome 1975, p. 219. Plate p. 220; Popoli anellenici in Basilicata,
    1971, p. 90f. Plate XXXV.

37. Valle di Pompei, Campania:
    M. Della Corte, 'Valle di Pompei. Parziale esplorazione di una villa
    rustica, nella cava di lapillo di Angelantonio De Martino', N.Sc. 1929,
    p. 190ff.

38. Via Tiberina, Roma:
    B.M. Felletti Maj., 'Roma (Via Tiberina) - villa rustica', N.Sc. 1955,
    pp. 206-16.

39. Vicovaro (Licenza), Lazio:
    G. Lugli, 'La villa Sabina di Orazio', M.A. XXXI (1926), p. 125ff,
    p. 502, No. 14; C.F. Giuliani, Tibur: part II. Forma Italiae Reg.
    I.3. Rome 1966, p. 74, No. 70. Fig. 73.

40. Villa Magna (Anagni), Lazio:
    M. Mazzolani, Anagnia: Forma Italiae Reg. I. Vol. 6., Rome 1969,
    pp. 133-8, No. 104; T. Ashby, 'The classical topography of the Roman
    Campagna - III (the Via Latina)', P.B.S.R. V (1910), p. 425.

41. Vittimose (Buccino), Campania:
    R. Ross Holloway and S.L. Dyson, 'Excavations at Buccino, 1970',
    A.J.A. 75. (1971), pp. 151-54; Ross Holloway, 'Villa romana',
    in Atti del IX convegno di studi sulla Magna Grecia, Napoli 1970,
    p. 203; S. Dyson, 'A Silenus mask mould from the excavations at
    Buccino (Salerno)', Arch. Class. XXIV (1972), pp. 269-82.

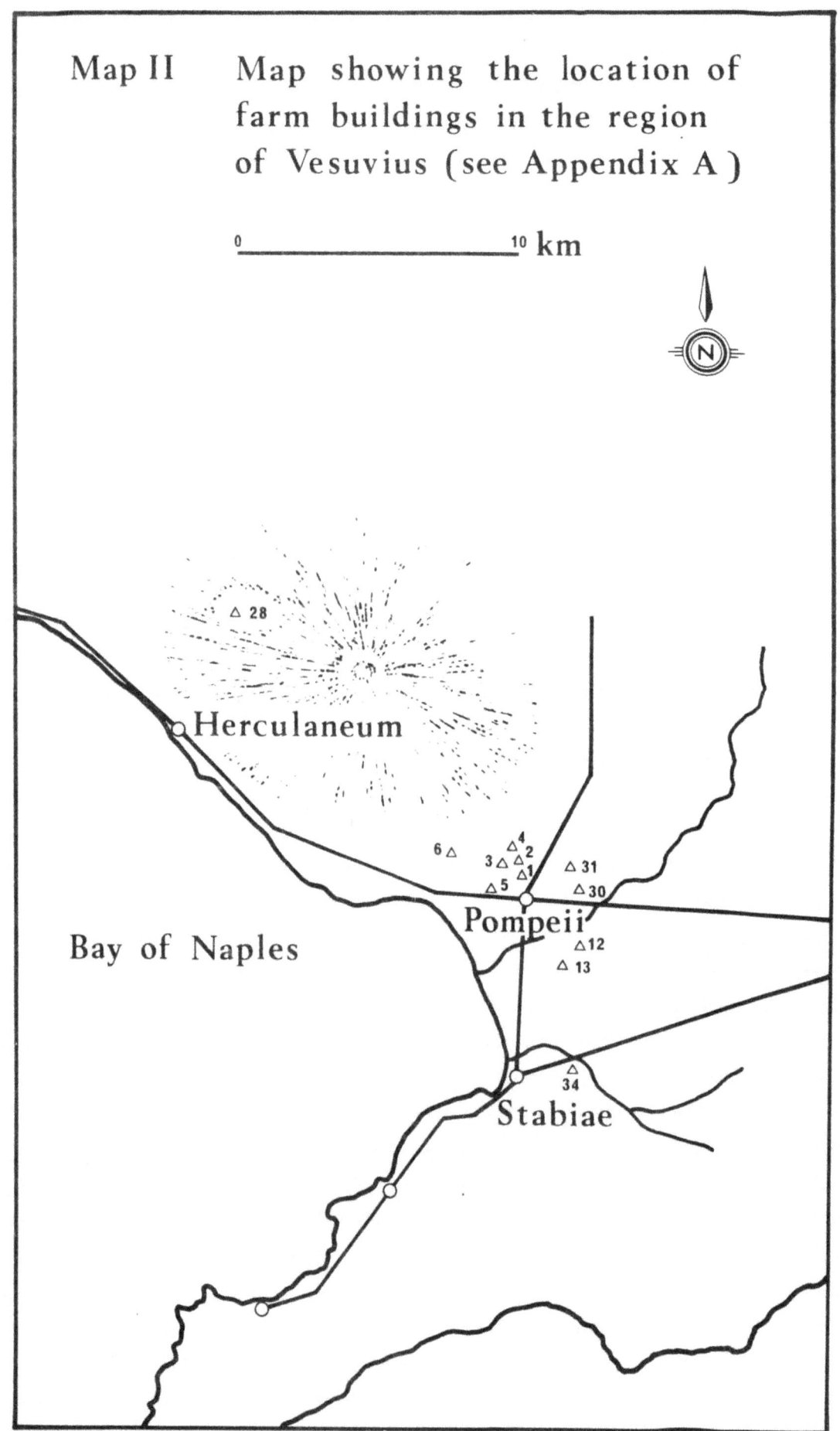

APPENDIX B

Other sites: a further catalogue of excavated (or surveyed) farm buildings.*

Akrai (Siracusa), Sicilia:
G. Gurcio, 'Akrai (Siracusa)—richerche nel territorio: la fattoria tardo-ellenistica', N.Sc. 1970, pp. 447-465.

Benzone (Collazia), Lazio:
L. Quilici, Collatia—Forma Italiae Reg. I. Vol. 10, Rome 1974, No. 106, pp. 242-5; R. Lanciani, N.Sc. 1883, pp. 169-70.

Casali di Mentana (Mentana), Lazio:
C. Pala, Nomentum—Forma Italiae Reg. 1. Vol. 12, Rome 1976, No. 1102, pp. 75-9.

Casignana (Bianco), Calabria:
G. Foti, Atti del V convegno di studi sulla Magna Grecia, Napoli 1966, p. 225f.

Cecchignola (Via Ardeatina), Roma:
P. E. Arias, 'Villa repubblicana presso La Cecchignola', N.Sc. 1939, pp. 351-60.

Colle Faustiniano (Praeneste), Lazio:
M. P. Muzzioli, Praeneste—Forma Italiae Reg. I. Vol. 8., Rome 1970, No. 106, 'Villa e cisterna', pp. 103-4.

Fiumana (Forlî), Emilia e Romagna:
G. Montanari, 'La villa romana di Fiumana' in G. Susini (ed), La Villa Romana', Faenza 1971, pp. 51-73.

Grotte S. Stefano (Viterbo), Lazio:
G. Colonna, 'Villa rustica e altri resti in localita Piani di Magugnano', N.Sc. 1975, pp. 53-8.

Livastrito (Cori), Lazio:
P. B. Vittucci, Cora—Forma Italiae Reg. I. Vol. 5., Rome 1968, no. 32, pp. 113-6.

Lucus Feroniae, Lazio:
R. Bandinelli and M. Torelli, L'Arte dell'Antichità Classica 2: Etruria Roma, Turin 1976, No. 65.

---

* This catalogue does not include the remaining 'Campanian villae rusticae' listed by J. Day, 'Agriculture in the life of Pompeii', Yale Classical Studies III (1932), Table C, pp. 202-3. The list is selective; it includes buildings that have been excavated, or those which have been surveyed to provide an adequate plan of their main features. It also contains references to recent excavations whose detailed publication may be forthcoming.

Luogosano (contrada S. Stefano), Campania:
E. Gabrici, 'Luogosano-avanzi di costruzioni di età romana sul Monte S. Stefano', N.Sc. 1901, pp. 333-6.

Macerata (Anagni), Lazio:
M. Mazzolani, Anagnia—Forma Italiae Reg. I. Vol. 6., Rome 1969, No. 35, pp. 113-4.

Mensa Matelica (Ravenna), Emilia e Romagna:
G. A. Mansuelli, 'Ravenna (frazione Mensa)—abitato preistorico. Casa romana', N.Sc. 1959, pp. 31-5.

Metauros (Sybaris), Calabria:
A. De Francescis, 'Metauros: la casa romana', A.M.S.M.G. III (1960), pp. 52-6.

Montecanino (Capena), Lazio:
M. Pallottino, 'Capena—resti di costruzioni romane e medioevali in località "Montecanino" ', N.Sc. 1937, pp. 7-28.

Monte Cuculo (Capena), Lazio:
G.D.B. Jones 'Capena and the Ager Capenas: Part I', P.B.S.R. XVII (1962) Site No. 204, p. 179.

Montegiardino (Collazia), Lazio:
L. Quilici, op.cit., No. 242, pp. 391-5, Figs. 842-5.

Nocera Superiore, Campania:
M. Della Corte, 'Nocera Superiore—piscina a ruderi di una villa rustica', N.Sc. 1932, pp. 318-9.

Orbetello, Lazio:
G. Maetzke, 'Villa rustica in tenuta Polverosa', N.Sc. 1958, pp. 34-49.

Pollena Trocchia, Campania:
M. Della Corte, 'Pollena Trocchia—cella vinaria e piscina presso i ruderi di una villa rustica', N.Sc. 1932, pp. 311-14.

Porto Saturo (Leporano), Puglia:
E. Lattanzi, in Atti del X convegno di studi sulla Magna Grecia, Napoli 1971, p. 541.

Pratigioli (Anagni), Lazio:
Mazzolani, op.cit., Nos. 76/79, pp. 124-5.

Punta della vipera (S. Marinella), Lazio:
M. Torelli, 'Terza campagna di scavi a Punta della Vipera (S.Marinella)' Studi Etruschi XXXV (1967), pp. 331-352.

Pyrgi, Lazio:
F. Castagnoli and L. Cozza, 'Appunti sulla topografia di Pyrgi', P.B.S.R. XXV (1957), pp. 16-21; p. 20 Fig. 2.

Riolo (Bologna), Emilia e Romagna:
A. Negrioli, 'Riolo—scoperte di costruzioni romane', N.Sc. 1913, pp. 202-4.

San Marino (Napoli), Campania:

A. Rocco, 'S. Rocco di Marano (Napoli)—ricognizione archeologica nella frazione di S. Rocco', N.Sc. 1954, p. 33ff.

Serrone (Anagni), Lazio:

Mazzolani, op.cit., No. 89, 'Villa rustica e terrazamenti agricoli al Serrone', pp. 128-9.

Torricella, Puglia:

F. G. Lo Porto, 'Resti di una villa rustica romana', Atti del XI convegno di studi sulla Magna Grecia, Napoli 1972, p. 500. Plate CXXXVIII.

Vagni (Buccino), Campania:

S. L. Dyson, 'Excavations at Buccino, 1971', A.J.A. 76 (1972), pp. 159-163.

BIBLIOGRAPHY

This bibliography does not contain the excavation reports of individual sites, which have been listed in Appendices A and B. It is a list of those works which have been consulted or cited in the notes. A further list of frequently cited works will be found under Abbreviations (pp. viii-x). I have excluded any works relating to villa studies outside Italy (they are far too numerous) unless they have been cited in the notes.

Adamesteanu, D. La Basilicata Antica. Salerno: Di Mauro, 1974.

Adamesteanu, D. 'La suddivisione di terra nel Metapontino' in Problemes de la Terre en Grece Ancienne. Ed. by M. I. Finley. Paris: Mouton, 1973.

Applebaum, S. 'Farms and their uses' in: The Agrarian History of England and Wales: Vol. I-II. Cambridge: U. P., 1972, pp. 151-205.

Bastet, F. L. 'Villa rustica in contrada Pisanella', Cronache Pompeiane (Rivista dell'Associazione Internazionale "Amici di Pompei") II (1976), pp. 112-143.

Berggren, E. 'A new approach to the closing centuries of Etruscan history', Arctos V (1967), pp. 29-43.

Blake, M. E. Ancient Roman Construction in Italy (3 vols). Washington: American Philosophical Society, 1947-73.

Blake, M. E. 'The pavements of the Roman buildings of the Republic and early Empire', M.A.A.R. VIII (1930), pp. 1-50.

Boethius, A. 'Remarks on the development of domestic architecture in Rome', A.J.A. 38 (1934), p. 158 ff.

Boethius, A. The Golden House of Nero. Ann Arbor, 1960.

Boethius, A. (et.al.) Etruscan Culture, Land and People. Svenska Institutet i Rom. New York: Columbia U. P., 1962.

Bradford, J. 'Siticulosa Apulia', Antiquity XX (1946), pp. 191-200.

Bradford, J. 'Buried landscapes in southern Italy', Antiquity XXIII (1949), pp. 58-72.

Bradford, J. 'The Apulian expedition: an interim report', Antiquity XXIV (1950), pp. 84-95.

Bradford, J. Ancient Landscapes. London: G. Bell and Sons, 1957.

Brehaut, E. Cato the Censor on farming. New York: Columbia U.P., 1933.

Cagiano De Azevedo, M. 'Ville rustiche tardo antiche in Occidente', Settimane di Spoleto XIII (1966), p. 663ff.

Cagnat, R. V. and Chapot, V. Manuel d'archéologie Romaine (2 Vols). Paris, 1916-20.

Camps-Fabrer, H. L'olivier et l'huile dans l'Afrique Romaine. Algiers, 1953.

Carrington, R. 'Notes on the building materials of Pompeii', J.R.S. XXIII (1933), pp. 125-138.

Carrington, R. 'The ancient Italian town house', Antiquity VII (1933), p. 133ff.

Carrington, R. Pompeii. Oxford: U.P., 1936.

Castaldi, F. 'La transformazione della villa rustica romana in rapporto alle condizioni dell'agricoltura', Ann.Ist.Sup.Disc.e Lett. S. Chiara in Napoli 1950.

D'Arms, J. H. Romans on the Bay of Naples. Cambridge, Mass: Harvard U.P., 1970.

Day, J. 'Agriculture in the life of Pompeii', Y.Cl.S III (1932), p. 167ff.

De Cou, H. F. Antiquities from Boscoreale in Field Museum of Natural History. Chicago, 1912.

Della Corte, M. Case ed abitanti di Pompei. Naples: Fausto Fiorentino, 1965.

Dioniso, F. Le ville di Orazio: la villa rurale del "Digentia" e la villa signorile di Tibur. Tivoli: Società di Villa d'Este, Atti e Memorie, 1966.

Dufkova, J. and Pecirka, J. 'Excavations of farms and farmhouses in the chora of Chersonesos', Eirene VIII (1970), pp. 123-174.

Duncan, G. 'Sutri: notes on southern Etruria 3', P.B.S.R. XIII (1958), pp. 63-134.

Duncan-Jones, R. The Economy of the Roman Empire: quantitative studies. Cambridge: U.P., 1974.

Eschebach, H. Die stadtebauliche Entwicklung des antiken Pompeji. Heidelberg, 1970.

Etienne, R. 'Recherches sur l'ergastule' in: Actes du colloque 1972 sur l'esclavage. Paris: Annales littéraires de l'Université de Besançon. Les Belles Lettres. 1974.

Fabbricotti, E. 'I bagni nelle prime ville romane', Cronache Pompeiane II (1976), pp. 29-111.

Frederiksen, M. W. 'The contribution of archaeology to the agrarian problem in the Gracchan period', Dialoghi di Archeologia, Anno IV - V (1970-1), Rome 1972.

Gentry, A. P. Roman Military Stone-Built Granaries in Britain. Oxford: B.A.R. 32. 1976.

Goujard, R. 'Etude critique de quelques passages de Caton, De Agricultura.' Revue de Philologie 46.2. (1972), pp. 266-74.

Graham, J. W. 'Origins and interrelationships of the Greek house and the Roman house', Phoenix XX (1966), pp. 3-31.

Grimal, P. 'Les maisons à tour hellénistiques et romaines', M.E.F.R. 56 (1939), pp. 28-59.

Grimal, P. Les Jardins Romains. (2nd ed.) Paris: Presses Universitaires de France, 1969.

Gummerus, H. 'Die Romische Gutsbetrieb als wirtschaftlicher Organismus nach den Werken des Cato, Varro und Columella', Klio I (Beiheft 5), 1906.

Harmand, J. 'Sur la valeur archéologique du mot "villa" ', Rev. Arch. XXXVIII (1951), pp. 155-8.

Jashemski, W. F. 'University of Maryland excavations at Pompeii, 1968', A.J.A. 74 (1970), pp. 62-7.

Jashemski, W. F. 'The discovery of a large vineyard at Pompeii: University of Maryland excavations, 1970', A.J.A. 77 (1973), pp. 27-41.

Jones, G. D. B. 'Capena and the Ager Capenas', P.B.S.R. XVII (1962), pp. 116-208, XVIII (1963), pp. 100-158.

Jones, J. E. 'The Dema house in Attica', B.S.A. LVII (1962), pp. 76-114.

Jones, J. E., Graham, A.J., and Sackett, L. H. 'An Attic country house below the cave of Pan at Vari', B.S.A. 68 (1973), pp. 355-452.

Jungst, E. and Thielscher, P. 'Catos Keltern und Kollergange', Bonn. Jahrb. 54 (1954), pp. 32-93.

Kahrstedt, U. 'Die Wirtschaftliche Lage Grossgriechenlands in der Kaiserzeit', Historia Einzelschrift No. 4 (1960).

Kent, J. H. 'The temple estates of Delos, Rheneia, and Mykonos', Hesperia XVII (1948), p. 243ff.

Lacava, M. Topografia e storia di Metaponto. Naples, 1891.

Lake, A. K. 'The origin of the Roman house', A.J.A. 41 (1937), pp. 592-601.

Lehmann, P. W. Roman wall paintings from Boscoreale in the Metropolitan Museum of Art. (Monographs of Archaeology and Fine Art V). Cambridge, Mass. 1953.

Ling, R. 'Studius and the beginnings of Roman landscape painting', J.R.S. LXVII (1977), pp. 1-16.

Lugli, G. La tecnica edilizia romana: con particolare riguardo a Roma e Lazio. (2 Vols). Rome: Giovanni Bardi, 1957.

Magaldi, E. Lucania Romana I, Rome: Istituto di Studi Romani, 1947.

Maiuri, A. La villa dei misteri (2 Vols). Rome: La libreria dello stato, 1947.

Mansuelli, G. A. 'La villa romana nell'Italia settentrionale', P.P. LVII (1957), pp. 444-458.

Mansuelli, G. A. Le ville nel mondo romano. Milan, 1958.

Mansuelli, G. A. 'La casa Etrusca di Marzabotto', Röm. Mitth. LXX (1963), pp. 44-62.

Mansuelli, G. A. Urbanistica e architettura della Cisalpina romana (Coll. Latomus III), Brussels: Latomus, 1971.

Martin, R. Recherches sur les Agronomes Latins. Paris: Belles Lettres, 1971.

Martin, R. 'Familia rustica: les esclaves chez les agronomes latins', in: Actes du colloque sur l'esclavage, 1972. Paris: Annales littéraires de l'Université de Besançon. Les Belles Lettres, 1974.

Mau, A. and Kelsey, F. W. Pompeii. Its life and Art. New York: Macmillan, 1899.

Maurin, L. 'Etablissement vinicole à Allas-les-mines', Gallia 22 (1964), pp. 218-21.

McDonald, A. H. Republican Rome. London: Thames and Hudson, 1966.

McKay, A. G. Houses, Villas and Palaces in the Roman World. London: Thames and Hudson, 1975.

Oates, D. 'The Tripolitanian Gebel: settlement of the Roman period around Gasr ed-Daun', P.B.S.R. XXI (1953), pp. 81-113.

Ogilvie, R. M. 'Eretum', P.B.S.R. XX (1965), p. 70ff.

Pecirka, J. 'Country estates of the polis of Chersonesos in the Crimea', in: Ricerche storiche ed economiche in memoria di Corrado Barbagallo I. Naples 1970, pp. 459-477.

Pecirka, J. 'Homestead farms in classical and hellenistic Hellas', in: Problèmes de la terre en Grèce ancienne. Ed. by M. I. Finley. Paris: Mouton, 1973.

Percival, J. The Roman Villa. London: Batsford, 1977.

Plommer, H. Vitruvius and later Roman Building manuals. Cambridge: U.P. 1973.

Ponsich, M. Recherches archéologiques à Tanger et dans sa région. Paris: C.N.S.R. 1970.

Precheur-Canonge, T. La vie rurale en Afrique Romaine d'après les mosaïques. Tunis: U.P., 1962.

Reinach, S. Répertoire de peintures grecques et romaines. (Reprint) Rome: L'Erma di Bretschneider, 1972.

Richardson, L. Jr. 'The Casa dei Dioscuri and its Painters', M.A.A.R. XXIII (1955).

Robinson, D. M. and Graham, J. W. Excavations at Olynthos, Part VIII: The Hellenic house. Baltimore: John Hopkins U.P., 1938.

Robinson, D. M. Excavations at Olynthos, Part XII: Domestic and public architecture. Baltimore: John Hopkins U.P. 1946.

Rostovtzeff, M. 'Pompeianische Landschaften und romische Villen', Jahrb. Deut. Arch. Inst. XIX (1904), pp. 10-126.

Rostovtzeff, M. 'Die hellenistich-römische Architekturlandschaft', Röm. Mitth. XXVI (1911), pp. 1-185.

Ruggiero, M. Degli Scavi di Stabia dal 1749 al 1782. Naples, 1881.

Salmon, E. T. Samnium and the Samnites. Cambridge: U.P., 1967.

Salmon, E. T. Roman Colonization under the Republic. London: Thames and Hudson, 1969.

Settis, S. 'Per l'interpretazione di Piazza Amerina', M.E.F.R. 87 (1975 - 2), pp. 873-994.

Sherwin-White, A. N. The Letters of Pliny. Oxford: U.P., 1966.

Sirago, V. A. L'Italia agraria sotto Traiano. Louvain: U.P., 1958.

Skydsgaard, J. E. Den Romerske Villa Rustica. (Studier fra sprog-og oldtidsforskning). Copenhagen, 1961.

Skydsgaard, J. E. 'Nuove ricerche sulla villa rustica romana fino all'epoca di Traiano', Analecta Romana Instituti Danici 5 (1969), pp. 25-40.

Stevens, C. E. 'Agriculture and rural life in the later Roman Empire', in: The Cambridge economic history of Europe: Vol. I. Ed. by J. H. Clapham and E. Power. Cambridge: U.P., 1966, pp. 89-117.

Stucchi, S. Forum Iulii (Cividale des Friuli), (Italia romana XI), Rome 1951.

Susini, G. (Ed.) La Villa Romana (Giornata di Studi). Faenza: Fratelli Lega, 1971.

Swoboda, K. Römische und romanische Palaste: eine architekturgeschichtliche Untersuchung. Vienna 1919.

Tamm, B. 'Some notes on Roman houses', Op.Rom. IX (1973), pp. 56-60.

Tibiletti, G. 'Lo sviluppo del latifondo in Italia dall'epoca Graccana al principio dell'impero', X Congresso Internazionale di Scienze Storiche. Rome 4-11 Sett. 1955: Vol. II. Florence 1955, p. 237ff.

Toynbee, A. Hannibal's Legacy. (2 Vols). Oxford: U.P., 1965.

Uggeri, G. 'ΚΛΗΡΟΙ arcaici e bonifica classica nella ΧΩΡΑ di Metaponto', P.P. CXXIV (1969), pp. 51-71.

Van Buren, A. W. 'Laurentinum Plinii Minoris', Rend. Pont. Acc. Arch. 20 (1943-4), pp. 165-192.

Van Buren, A. W. 'Pliny's Laurentine villa', J.R.S. XXXVIII (1948), pp. 35-6.

Vinson, P. 'Ancient roads between Venosa and Gravina', P.B.S.R. XXVII (1972), pp. 165-192.

White, K. D. 'Latifundia', Bull. Inst. Class. Stud. 14 (1967), pp. 62-79.

White, K. D. A bibliography of Roman agriculture. Reading: Institute of Agricultural history, 1970.

White, K. D. 'Roman agricultural writers I: Varro and his predecessors', in: Aufsteig und Niedergang der Romischen Welt: Band IV. Ed. by H. Temporini and W. Haase. Berlin: Walter De Gruyter, 1973.

Yeo, C. 'The economics of Roman and American slavery', Finanzarchiv XIII (1952), p. 445ff.

Young, J. H. 'Studies in south Attica: country estates at Sounion', Hesp. XXV (1956), pp. 122-46.

Young, J. H. 'Ancient towers on the island of Siphnos', A.J.A. XL (1956), pp. 51-5.

www.ingramcontent.com/pod-product-compliance
Lightning Source LLC
Chambersburg PA
CBHW061539010526
44112CB00023B/2897